First World War
and Army of Occupation
War Diary
France, Belgium and Germany

40 DIVISION
Headquarters, Branches and Services
Royal Army Veterinary Corps
Assistant Director Veterinary Services
3 June 1916 - 16 March 1919

WO95/2597/4

Published by

The Naval & Military Press Ltd

Unit 10 Ridgewood Industrial Park,

Uckfield, East Sussex,

TN22 5QE England

Tel: +44 (0) 1825 749494

www.naval-military-press.com

www.nmarchive.com

This diary has been reprinted in facsimile from the original. Any imperfections are inevitably reproduced and the quality may fall short of modern type and cartographic standards.

© **Crown Copyright**
Images reproduced by permission of The National Archives, London, England, 2015.

Contents

Document type	Place/Title	Date From	Date To
Heading	WO95/2597/ 4		
Heading	Asst Dir. Veterinary Serv. Jun 1916-Mar 1919		
War Diary	Havre	03/06/1916	04/06/1916
War Diary	Lillers	05/06/1916	05/06/1916
War Diary	Norrent Fontes	06/06/1916	19/06/1916
War Diary	Bruay	20/06/1916	30/06/1916
Heading	War Diary Of Major. W. N. Rowston Avc A.V.C. A.D.V.S. 40th Div For July 1916		
War Diary	Bruay	01/07/1916	04/07/1916
War Diary	Noeux	05/07/1916	31/07/1916
Miscellaneous	War Diaries Of Major. W.N. Rowston A.D.V.S. 40th Division		
War Diary	Noeux	01/08/1916	31/08/1916
Miscellaneous	War Diaries Major W.N. Rowston A.V.C. A.D.V.S. 40th Division		
War Diary	Noeux	01/09/1916	29/10/1916
War Diary	Rollecourt	30/10/1916	04/11/1916
War Diary	Frohen Le Grand	03/11/1916	03/11/1916
War Diary	Bernaville	06/11/1916	15/11/1916
War Diary	Frohen Le Grand	16/11/1916	19/11/1916
War Diary	Bouquemaison	20/11/1916	22/11/1916
War Diary	Doullens	23/11/1916	23/11/1916
War Diary	Canaples	24/11/1916	24/11/1916
War Diary	Ailly Le Haut Clocher	25/11/1916	15/12/1916
War Diary	Ailly Le H.C.	15/12/1916	15/12/1916
War Diary	Chipilly	16/12/1916	28/12/1916
War Diary	L.16.d.1.9 (Bray)	29/12/1916	31/12/1916
War Diary	L 16.d.1.9 (Ailly Le Haut Sheet M Bray)	01/01/1917	05/01/1917
War Diary	L.16.d.1.9 M Bray	06/01/1917	31/01/1917
War Diary	Corbie	01/02/1917	12/02/1917
War Diary	Nr Bray	15/02/1917	08/03/1917
War Diary	Suzanne	09/03/1917	21/03/1917
War Diary	Curlu	22/03/1917	24/03/1917
War Diary	P C Craniere	25/03/1917	31/03/1917
Miscellaneous	On His Majesty's Service.		
War Diary	P C Craniere (Maurice)	01/04/1917	04/04/1917
War Diary	P C Craniere	05/04/1917	13/04/1917
War Diary	Manancourt	14/04/1917	30/04/1917
Heading	War Diaries Of Major. W.N. Rowston A.V.C. A.D.V.S. 40th Division May 1/31st 1917		
War Diary	Manancourt	01/05/1917	25/06/1917
Heading	War Diary Of D.A.D.V.S. 40th Division July 1/31st 1917		
War Diary	Manancourt	07/07/1917	11/07/1917
War Diary	Sorel	12/07/1917	01/08/1917
War Diary	Sorel Le Grand Sheet 57 C V18.d.5.7	01/08/1917	08/08/1917
War Diary	Sorel Le Grand	09/08/1917	15/08/1917
War Diary	Sorel	16/08/1917	31/08/1917
War Diary	Sorel Le Grand V18.d.5.7 (Sheet 57 C)	01/09/1917	04/09/1917
War Diary	Sorel Le Grand	04/09/1917	17/09/1917

War Diary	Sorel	18/09/1917	30/09/1917
War Diary	Sorel V18.d.5.7 Sheet 57 C	01/10/1917	08/10/1917
War Diary	Fosseux P10 Sheet 57 C	09/10/1917	16/10/1917
War Diary	Fosseux	17/10/1917	28/10/1917
War Diary	Lucheux T16 Sheet 51 C	29/10/1917	06/11/1917
War Diary	Lucheux	08/11/1917	16/11/1917
War Diary	Fosseux	17/11/1917	17/11/1917
War Diary	Achiet Le Petit G14/ Sh 57 C)	18/11/1917	18/11/1917
War Diary	Haplincourt O 3 (57 C)	19/11/1917	19/11/1917
War Diary	Haplincourt	20/11/1917	22/11/1917
War Diary	Neuville	23/11/1917	27/11/1917
War Diary	Basseux (lens 1-100000)	28/11/1917	02/12/1917
War Diary	Behagnies	03/12/1917	13/12/1917
War Diary	Gomiecourt (A 29 Sheet 57 C)	14/12/1917	16/12/1917
War Diary	Gomiecourt	17/12/1917	31/12/1917
War Diary	Gomiecourt A 79 Sheet 57c	01/01/1918	06/01/1918
War Diary	Behagnies H2 Sheet 57c	07/01/1918	08/01/1918
War Diary	Behagnies	08/01/1918	21/01/1918
War Diary	Behagnies (H.2. Sheet 57 C)	06/02/1918	12/02/1918
War Diary	Gomiecourt (A 29. St 57 C)	13/02/1918	18/02/1918
War Diary	Gomiecourt	19/02/1918	28/02/1918
War Diary	Basseux (map Ref Lens II)	01/03/1918	07/03/1918
War Diary	Basseux	08/03/1918	22/03/1918
War Diary	Bucquoy	23/03/1918	23/03/1918
War Diary	Souastre	24/03/1918	28/03/1918
War Diary	Lucheux	29/03/1918	29/03/1918
War Diary	Chelers	30/03/1918	31/03/1918
War Diary	Merville (Sheet Hazebrouck 5A)	01/04/1918	02/04/1918
War Diary	Croix Du Bac (Sheet 36 G. 6c)	03/04/1918	07/04/1918
War Diary	Croix Du Bac	08/04/1918	09/04/1918
War Diary	La Motte Au Bois	10/04/1918	11/04/1918
War Diary	Au Souverain	13/04/1918	13/04/1918
War Diary	Renescure	14/04/1918	14/04/1918
War Diary	Longuenesse	15/04/1918	16/04/1918
War Diary	Wizernes	17/04/1918	30/04/1918
War Diary	St Omer	01/05/1918	03/06/1918
War Diary	Lederzeele 27/b 28a	04/06/1918	08/06/1918
War Diary	Lederzeele	09/06/1918	23/06/1918
War Diary	Renescure	24/06/1918	30/06/1918
War Diary	Renescure Sht 27 T.20d.	01/07/1918	08/07/1918
War Diary	Renescure	09/07/1918	31/07/1918
War Diary	Renescure Sht 27 T.20.d.	01/08/1918	08/08/1918
War Diary	Renescure	09/08/1918	23/08/1918
War Diary	Wallon Cappel 27/U 29	24/08/1918	25/08/1918
War Diary	Wallon-Cappel	26/08/1918	02/09/1918
War Diary	La Motte Au Bois 36A/D 30	03/09/1918	06/09/1918
War Diary	La Motte Au Bois	07/09/1918	30/09/1918
War Diary	Le Verrier	01/10/1918	17/10/1918
War Diary	Armentiers	18/10/1918	20/10/1918
War Diary	Mouvaux 36/F21d.57	21/10/1918	26/10/1918
War Diary	Lannoy	27/10/1918	31/10/1918
War Diary	Lannoy (nr Roubaix)	01/11/1918	18/11/1918
War Diary	Lannoy	09/11/1918	24/11/1918
War Diary	Roubaix	25/11/1918	16/03/1919

W 05/25/07 4:59 PM

40TH DIVISION

ASST DIR. VETERINARY SERV.
JUN 1916 - MAR 1919

40TH DIVISION

Army. Form C. 2118

ADVS 402

WAR DIARY
or
INTELLIGENCE SUMMARY
(Erase heading not required.)

Instructions regarding War Diaries and Intelligence Summaries are contained in F.S. Regs., Part II. and the Staff Manual respectively. Title Pages will be prepared in manuscript.

Place	Date	Hour	Summary of Events and Information	Remarks and references to Appendices
HAVRE	3/6/16	11 am	Arrived from Southampton on Ch.y.y. Bavaria	
"	4/6/16		Left HAVRE by train in night for LILLERS	
LILLERS	5/6/16	8 am	Arrived and proceeded to billeting area at NORRENT-FONTES.	
NORRENT-FONTES	6/6/16		Allotted certain strays to act spare, reported to DDVS Ineulair when horses from them were now to be evacuated to	
			Writes with billets in the village & inspected their horses	
	7/6/16		Wrote 51 MVS at AMETTES and arranged to move it to a new available spot more central, also wrote & gave to DM K.y.	
			Sent out standing orders to all VOs & instruction as to duties & returns	
	8/6/16		9 motor lorries sent to all VOs in case of unheralded & them unforeseeable	
			Their hire & damage	
			Issued instruction to OC MVS re duties, returns &c	
	9/6/16		Moved with A.D.C. from Mont and to 6th Cavalry & Base	
			Orders 40 D.A.C. at NEDON, NEDONCHELLE	
			Instructions issued to OC 51 M.V.S. to move the section to LA GORGUE	

Army Form C. 2118

WAR DIARY
or
INTELLIGENCE SUMMARY
(Erase heading not required.)

Instructions regarding War Diaries and Intelligence Summaries are contained in F. S. Regs, Part II. and the Staff Manual respectively. Title Pages. will be prepared in manuscript.

Place	Date	Hour	Summary of Events and Information	Remarks and references to Appendices
NORRENT-FONTES	1/6/16		Visited 185 & 181 Bde R.F.A. & inspected carts, horses & ambulances. V.O.'s on to procure in exchange of animals unable to proceed. Return from the march completed; inspected M.V.S. in its new billets at LA BOULÉE	
"	2/6/16		Particulars of units attached for evacuation to 1st, 15th & 16 Divisions sent to A.D.V.S. unconnected. Establishments reinforcements cleared up. Route A.D.V.S. 16 Div to convoy for units charge of units attached for evacuation	
"	3/6/16		Inspected horses at M.V.S. awaiting evacuation	
"	4/6/16		Arranged to evacuate animals of 12 Div which the M.V.S. of this division now unable to deal with owing to their approaching move	
"	5/6/16		Visited cooks of ants today	
"	6/6/16		Visited Div Train at LILLERS, 121st Bde at HAM-en-ARTOIS Inspected 46 Div Cavalry at FEBRIN PALFART A.D.S. C. died owing in relief of A.V.C. died on longer allowed	

Army. Form C. 2118

WAR DIARY
or
INTELLIGENCE SUMMARY
(Erase heading not required.)

Instructions regarding War Diaries and Intelligence Summaries are contained in F. S. Regs., Part II. and the Staff Manual respectively. Title Pages will be prepared in manuscript.

Place	Date	Hour	Summary of Events and Information	Remarks and references to Appendices
NORRENT FONTES	18/6/16		43 horses evacuated to rest hospital at NEUCHATEL	
	19/6/16		Div. H.Q. moved to BRUAY, the M.V. Section also billeted in BRUAY	
BRUAY	20/6/16		Inspected Mobile Vety section & various A.S.C., R.E. & Div. H.Q. animals billeted in BRUAY. Arrange to hold a stock of medicines on hand in case of emergency.	
BRUAY	21/6/16		Visited all billeting areas the inspect and horses left behind by units of the division which were reported unfit to be moved. Arrange for the destruction of two disposed to the base have horses at LILLERS	
"	22/6/16		Visited Field Ambulances, A.S.C. Gave views to Capt. Islandwith known to Anglican and pulled to Transport, Royal Vety College, LONDON	
	23/6/16		Telegram received from Capt. B. C. LANCASTER M.V.C.(S.R.) to in S.I. MOBILE VETY. SECTION	
"	24/6/16		Inspected vans of mercury in m.o. Div Signal L.R.E. inspected all animals and arranged for dressing of mudsick with calomel ointment	

1875 Wt. W593/826 1,000,000 4/15 J.B.C. & A. A.D.S.S./Forms/C. 2118.

Army Form C. 2118

WAR DIARY
or
INTELLIGENCE SUMMARY
(Erase heading not required.)

Instructions regarding War Diaries and Intelligence Summaries are contained in F.S. Regs., Part II. and the Staff Manual respectively. Title Pages will be prepared in manuscript.

Place	Date	Hour	Summary of Events and Information	Remarks and references to Appendices
BRUAY	23/8/16		Completed & checked all equipment in charge of 51 MOBILE V.S. SECTION V.O. i/c 41st Div. ASC took over temporary charge of 51 M.V.S	
"	26/8/16		Capt EDWARDS AVC (SR) left for ENGLAND Completed horse of 119 Bde of Division 8 horses & 1 mule of this division evacuated to 51 MVS	
"	27/8/16		Capt. LANCASTER took over charge of 51 M.V.S. Orders received from D.D.V.S. 1st Army to test all horses of this division with intra-dermal malleine test; syringe & malleine (French) received	
"	28/8/16		Visited A.D.V.S. 16 Div to arrange for demonstration of intra-dermal malleine test to F.P. V.Os. of this Division could not however be arranged	
"	29/8/16 30/8/16		Completed Insp. of G.A.S.C. & 224th by R.E. & RUITZ Inspected horses of 119 Bde of Division	

W M Rowlands?
Major
ADVS? 41 Div

40 of July

War Diary of Major. W.N. ROWSTON. A.D.V.S. 40 Div.
A.V.C.
A.D.V.S. 40" DIV.

for July 1916

A.D.V.S. 40 Div
Vol 2

WAR DIARY or INTELLIGENCE SUMMARY

Army Form C. 2118

Place	Date	Hour	Summary of Events and Information	Remarks and references to Appendices
BRUAY	1/1/16		Demonstration given to U.O's with R.A. Units on method of carrying out into dismit. helpful mullein test at 2nd army M.U.S at MUEUX LE MINE. 9 and spent syringe + mullein to S.M.O's schools. Infantile fulminans anemia under mullein test – 40 Div. SIGNAL O. 136 F. AMBULANCE. 51 M.U.S. Weekly return & list of animals attached from schedule for the current week forwarded to D.D.V.S 1st Army	
"	2/1/16		Inspected animals under mullein test of 1 Div. Hqrs. 120 -- M.G. Coy. 229 F. Coy R.E. 2no 3 Coy A.S.C. Visited A.D.V.S 1st Div. to arrange for exchange of officer i/c + also for M.U.S and coherence villeting attention in the Div. divram exchanging area.	
"	3/1/16		On mule of 40th Signal Co. which showed signs of reaction to mullein moved to M.U.S & detailed track to unknown mullein to in the other couple with next helpful test.	

WAR DIARY
or
INTELLIGENCE SUMMARY

Army Form C. 2118

(Erase heading not required.)

Place	Date	Hour	Summary of Events and Information	Remarks and references to Appendices
NOEUX	4/7/16		Dn. H.Q. moved to NOEUX LES MINES. 51 M.V.S. moved to DROUVIN. Mules reported to us ends of 3/7/16 did not rest on 2nd testing.	
"	6/7/16		Under M.V.S. at DROUVIN & inspected kettle & attendering. Not heard how of remounts at NOEUX station & supervise the detrainment & distribution of 59 remounts.	
"	7/7/16		D.D.V.S. & D.D.R. 1st Army went round horses of 1F, 27/I Bde R.F.A. Saw their horses to be evacuated; few animals to be remounts as remount cases. On case in C.178 supervision of mange; advise to be isolated & evacuated to M.V.S. Afternoon spent in checking & completing mouth returns & readings return. Afternoon went round no 4 Section D.A.C. at HESDIGNEUL. Two debility, serve (mules) and three close to be evacuated. Inspection A.S.C. horses under within list.	

Army Form C. 2118

WAR DIARY
or
INTELLIGENCE SUMMARY
(Erase heading not required.)

Instructions regarding War Diaries and Intelligence Summaries are contained in F.S. Regs., Part II. and the Staff Manual respectively. Title Pages will be prepared in manuscript.

Place	Date	Hour	Summary of Events and Information	Remarks and references to Appendices
NOEUX	8/1/16		All outstanding examinations for the month cleared up & the month return despatched. Visited LES BREBIS & ascertained the whereabouts of the horse gunshot stores. Inspected animals of 181 Bde R.F.A. under test with gunshot stores. Imputed arrival of 181 Bde R.F.A. under test. The picketing mud has been very wet & churned all of the horse lines have been in a bad state. Twenty seven animals examined sterling ather no 51 M.V.S.	
"	9/1/16		Went round 181 Bde R.F.A. & picked out horses for evacuation for debility. Imputed horses under mallein test r 185 & 198 Bde R.F.A. also picked out debilitated cases in 2 batteries of 185 Bde R.F.A.	
"	10		Went round 178 Bde R.F.A. & picked out horses for evacuation for debility.	

1875 Wt. W593/826 1,000,000 4/15 J.B.C. & A. A.D.S.S./Forms/C.2118.

WAR DIARY
or
INTELLIGENCE SUMMARY
(Erase heading not required.)

Army Form C. 2118

Place	Date	Hour	Summary of Events and Information	Remarks and references to Appendices
NOEUX	10/7/16		Inspected horses under mallein test in No 3 Section 40 D.A.C	
	11/7/16		Went round 188 Bde R.F.A. & pulled out sick mules. Took horses of the Brigade as all on the line out. Also Inspected horses under mallein test in No 2 Section 40 D.A.C	
	12/7/16		Went round 2 batteries of 185 Bde. R.F.A. & inspected animals under mallein test & also pulled out the horses for evacuation. Inspected animals under mallein test in Div Train. Their line been evacuated by M.V.S.	
	13/7/16		Inspected horses of 1 R.E Field Companies at LES BREBIS. Inspected 2 section of D.A.C. under mallein test	
	14/7/16		Horses afoot in sheltering returns. Inspected No 4 Section D.A.C. under mallein test.	

1875 Wt. W593/826 1,000,000 4/15 J.B.C. & A. A.D.S.S./Forms/C. 2118.

WAR DIARY or INTELLIGENCE SUMMARY

Army Form C. 2118

Place	Date	Hour	Summary of Events and Information	Remarks and references to Appendices
NOEUX	15/9/16		Report submitted to D.A.Q.M.G. re condition of the horses in the divisional rg'n in R.A. & Div. Train; recommendation made re green forage, shift & making use of am. grass on derelict land in the forward area.	
	16/9/16		Visited transport lines of 119th M. Bde.; horses on the whole in good condition; mean of the mules in too rather poor condition; have brought this to the notice of Brigade transport officer; care must be exercised that mules aft. their full ration. Forty two horses (much debility cases) evacuated by 31 M V S	
	19/9/16		Went round No. 2 sub Coy Div. Train; a number of aged horses which should be replaced so unable to work regularly & maintain their condition. Other animals in fair working order though rather light in condition.	

WAR DIARY
or
INTELLIGENCE SUMMARY

Army Form C. 2118

Place	Date	Hour	Summary of Events and Information	Remarks and references to Appendices
NOEUX	18/9/16		Inspected transport animals of 170 Inf: Bde; horses on the whole in good condition. Accompanied D.D.R. & D.D.V.S 1st Army on their inspection of 40th Div: Truvin; a number of aged & poor animals in No 2 Coy; shown in No 4 Company require more supervision.	
	19/9/16		Inspected standing clothes for advanced collecting station at LE BBE B'S Inspected No 51 Motl: V: Section. Rest of day to inspections on routine & office work. Towards there not been are notices by 51 M.V.S	
	20/9/16		Insp d tr transport animals of 171 Inf. Bde; condition on the whole good all round; shoeing neglected in some cases; informed staff capthe of this.	

Army Form C. 2118

WAR DIARY
or
INTELLIGENCE SUMMARY

(Erase heading not required.)

Instructions regarding War Diaries and Intelligence Summaries are contained in F. S. Regs., Part II. and the Staff Manual respectively. Title Pages will be prepared in manuscript.

Place	Date	Hour	Summary of Events and Information	Remarks and references to Appendices
NOEUX	21/4/16	a.m.	Met engagement of remounts for No Div & arranged for their distribution. Morning spent in completing returns & routine correspondence. Afternoon visited 40th D.A.C. to inspect case of influenza mange, & taken remount in to investigate & dispose of suspected case.	
	22/4/16		Weather returns read in also test of medical history of the whole of the workmen. All attendance correspondence for the week cleared up.	
	23/4/16		Inspected horses of D.185 Bde. R.F.A. for skin disease; no animal to g.t. M.V.S.; and others to be kept under observation. Visited 51 M.V.S.; arranged for a supply of calcium sulphate & medicine solution to be always kept on hand.	

1875 Wt. W593/826 1,000,000 4/15 J.B.C. & A. A.D.S.S./Forms/C. 2118.

WAR DIARY or INTELLIGENCE SUMMARY

Army Form C. 2118

Place	Date	Hour	Summary of Events and Information	Remarks and references to Appendices
MOEUX	24/4/16		Inspected D/181 Bde R.F.A., pastern animals in light condition; one mule I heard cab recommended for these animals for a fortnight. Went round transport animals of 119 of 2nd Bde; showing of some of the transport animals not good; the feet very long; this most noticeable in 19 W.H. & 19 R.W. Fusiliers & Bde Head quarters; notified Bde Head quarters and notified them to detail captain. Visited No. 1 Co. No Divn Train. Nine horse casualties today by M.V.S.	
	25/4/16		Inspected horses of 19th Bde R.F.A., on the whole a general improvement over last inspection.	
	26/4/16		Inspected horses of 188 Bde R.F.A.; still a great deal of room for improvement. Shod horses on the march in the division arranged to the attention over to get horses cob in addition to the ordinary rations. Inspected No 51 M.D.S.	

Army Form C. 2118

WAR DIARY
or
INTELLIGENCE SUMMARY
(Erase heading not required.)

Instructions regarding War Diaries and Intelligence Summaries are contained in F. S. Regs., Part II. and the Staff Manual respectively. Title Pages will be prepared in manuscript.

Place	Date	Hour	Summary of Events and Information	Remarks and references to Appendices
NOEUX	27/9/16		Went round horses of his batteries (A.B) 181 Bde R.F.A. picked out animals requiring an issue of linseed cake. Met DDR & DDVS 1st Army at Three Huts of No Dn Train who was inspecting H.Q. horses to be returned to No 1 Remount Section. Afternoon spent in routine office work & correspondence.	
	28/9/16		Weekly return of different units received checked & weekly returns completed. Went round horses of C 181 Bde picked out other horses for evacuation and three regiments an issue of linseed cake. Met remount train at NOEUX & supervised distribution of 6 G remounts to N.O Dnvin. Twenty one casos evacuated by 51 M.V.S.	

WAR DIARY
or
INTELLIGENCE SUMMARY
(Erase heading not required.)

Army Form C. 2118

Place	Date	Hour	Summary of Events and Information	Remarks and references to Appendices
NOEUX	29/9/16		All attendance correspondence & Office work for the preceding week cleared up; return for the week dispatched.	
	30/9/16		Under 185 Bde R.F.A., route impulses aid & them have prepared for evacuation. Twenty two cases evacuated to 51 M.U.S.	
	31/9/16		During this month 143 horses have been evacuated from the division for sick reasons. Of these 87 were debility cases divided as follows: from R.A. 73; R.E. 2; Inf. Transport 8; A.S.C. 4. The other 56 cases are from the following: R.A. 31; R.E. 1; Infantry Transport 11; A.S.C. 13. The condition of the horses has improved on the whole though there is still room for improvement in some of the R.O. Units.	

War Diaries of:-

Major. W. N. Rowsham. A.D.V.S., 40th Division.

Capt: G. C. Lancaster. O.C., 51st M.V.S.

From August 1st to 31st 1916.

Army Form C. 2118

A D V S

VOL 3

WAR DIARY
or
INTELLIGENCE SUMMARY
(Erase heading not required.)

Place	Date	Hour	Summary of Events and Information	Remarks and references to Appendices
NOEUX	1/8/16		Attended inspection by G.O.C. 1st Corps of horses of 1st Divs: Artillery & No Div: Train	
	2/8/16		Went round horses of 120th Inf. Bde.; shoeing of 1st M.A.S. Highlander & 120 Machine Gun Co. not satisfactory; test in many cases much too long; drew attention of Bde Transport officer to this. Visited 51 M.V.S.; letter arrangement as necessary than in regard to men, food & flag petroleum	
	3/8/16		Met D.D.V.S. at BETHUNE re evacuation of horses by barge; saw the first barge-load shipped and sent off; decided that if him drawn in BETHUNE shall make use of the awaited; the drawn to help them to fill up to its numbers required to fill barge when necessary	

WAR DIARY
or
INTELLIGENCE SUMMARY
(Erase heading not required.)

Army Form C. 2118

Instructions regarding War Diaries and Intelligence Summaries are contained in F. S. Regs., Part II. and the Staff Manual respectively. Title Pages will be prepared in manuscript.

Place	Date	Hour	Summary of Events and Information	Remarks and references to Appendices
NOEUX	4/8/16		Morning spent in checking & examining returns for the week & in comparing candidates returns. Met & remarks at NOEUX station & arranged distribution.	
NOEUX	5/8/16		Went round horses of 121 Inf Bde; condition of horses good on whole but showing apt to be neglected after too long a trek. M.B. & Mules are all built about a stone debtles management is not good, & their standings ought to be better kept, there & things are greater out to the officer concerned. Inspected animals in S.I.M.V.S. awaiting evacuation.	
	6/8/16		Attended conference held by D.D.V.S. 1st Army at 1st Army Head Quarters. 1 wounds on animal evacuated to 51 M.V.S	

Army Form C. 2118

WAR DIARY
or
INTELLIGENCE SUMMARY
(Erase heading not required.)

Instructions regarding War Diaries and Intelligence Summaries are contained in F. S. Regs., Part II. and the Staff Manual respectively. Title Pages will be prepared in manuscript.

Place	Date	Hour	Summary of Events and Information	Remarks and references to Appendices
NOEUX	7/8/16		Arranged with O/C for a call above to be sent temporarily to each of the M.G. Corps till they can leave & send men of their own. Returned D.A.G.M.S. on the subject kept animals being returned to remount section, draft notes published on the subject all animals to be unfit for V.O. before sending them to remounts.	
	8/8/16		German correspondence & routine work. Visited 51 M.V.S. and inspected horses for evacuation.	
	9/8/16		Visited No. 11 Section 40 D.A.C at HESDIGNEUL to an inspects case of mange in mule, animal evacuated by 51 MVS. Eleven animals evacuated by 51 MVS.	
	10/8/16		Visited unit of 40 Div. RE inspected all animals, shoeing in no. 3 Coy. Co. not as good as it should be; fitting tin long & very edges of shoe being road in own case. The other feet up in fairly good order; shoeing condition & general condition of animals good.	

Army Form C. 2118

WAR DIARY
or
INTELLIGENCE SUMMARY
(Erase heading not required.)

Place	Date	Hour	Summary of Events and Information	Remarks and references to Appendices
MOEUX	11/8/16		Spent in checking return from VO's & in completing medical returns & in routine correspondence	
	12/8/16		Visited No Du Train No 1 Coy to ascertain 2 horse ambulance arrange (one to be evacuated). Visited 18th Bde R.F.A. to ascertain 2 horse ambulance & arrange. Visited 51 M.V.S. to ascertain animal wounding evacuation	
	13/8/16		Office work & completing of return re duties of A.D.V.S. called for by D.V.S. 15 animal evacuated by 51 M.V.S.	
	14/8/16		Office work & routine correspondence	
	15/8/16		Visited infantile transport lines at LES BREBIS to ascertain amount of damage done by the hostile shelling on that day.	

Army Form C. 2118

WAR DIARY
or
INTELLIGENCE SUMMARY
(Erase heading not required.)

Instructions regarding War Diaries and Intelligence Summaries are contained in F.S. Regs., Part II. and the Staff Manual respectively. Title Pages will be prepared in manuscript.

Place	Date	Hour	Summary of Events and Information	Remarks and references to Appendices
NOEUX	16/8/16		Officer roll. Unites 51 M.V.S. & impulite cases awaiting evacuation	
	17/8/16		Impulits transport convoy of 135 & 136 F.Os Combs at LABEUVRIERE arrived in good condition & everything satisfactory. Net & average detentation of 28 arrived at NOEUX station	
	18/8/16		All V.O.'s & Officers next return & morning report in checking arms. Unites transport lines 119 & 120, 9nd Bde to input ampute. Cases. Sent apart to D.A.Q.M.S. recommending that transport Officers shall be published to exchange arms therefrom within authority. Am general with ampute cases driven hence own exchange in this way return to V.O.	
	19/8/16		Weekly return completed & forwarded. Imputits convoy for evacuation to M.V.S. Graham case trained by M.V.S.	

Army Form C. 2118

WAR DIARY
or
INTELLIGENCE SUMMARY
(Erase heading not required.)

Instructions regarding War Diaries and Intelligence Summaries are contained in F. S. Regs., Part II. and the Staff Manual respectively. Title Pages will be prepared in manuscript.

Place	Date	Hour	Summary of Events and Information	Remarks and references to Appendices
NOEUX	20/8/16		Visited No D.A.C. to inspect ammunition for whom an issue of horses etc has been demanded. Attended notification of ammunition prepared for evacuation on removal cases & arranged D.D.R. as required. Office work	
	21/8/16		Ambulance horses of 178 Bde R.F.A: condition fair & good. Met & arranged distribution of ammunition of removal of NOEUX station. Visited M.V.S. and inspected ammunition for evacuation.	
	22/8/16		Ambulance horses of 188 Bde R.F.A: condition moderate, arrangements for issue of horses etc to the next ones. Afternoon spent in office work	
	24/8/16		Visited BETHUNE to see ammunition evacuated & Major L STOMER. Visited for clear arrivals by train to 51 M.V.S	

Army Form C. 2118

WAR DIARY
or
INTELLIGENCE SUMMARY
(Erase heading not required.)

Instructions regarding War Diaries and Intelligence Summaries are contained in F. S. Regs., Part II. and the Staff Manual respectively. Title Pages will be prepared in manuscript.

Place	Date	Hour	Summary of Events and Information	Remarks and references to Appendices
MERVILLE	25/8/16		All U.O.'s at office; much return checked & compiled	
	26/8/16		Went return forwarded to DDVS 1st Army. Inspected horses of 181 Bde R.F.A.; condition unable; arranged one of limited cots for sterner amounts. Visited 51 M.V.S. to inspect animals awaiting evacuation	
	27/8/16		Sunday and nothing to record	
	28/8/16		Inspected transport animals of 119 2nd Bde; condition good in the whole though some unrest on tin item; showing in better hit items in old comdrill room for improvement	
	29/8/16		Visits BETHUNE to see animal wounded by burst. Went round 185 Bde R.F.A.; B & C Batteries have a large number of them horses showing on hoof; further inspection out 28 cases of evacuation. The other two batteries are satisfactory.	

WAR DIARY
or
INTELLIGENCE SUMMARY

Army Form C. 2118

Place	Date	Hour	Summary of Events and Information	Remarks and references to Appendices
NOEUX	30/8/16		Officer went, been revn all day	
	31/8/16		Infantry machine gunners of 40 Div R.A. which have been employed on attachment, this unit for recover in event of firm evacuation out & M.V.S. D.V.S. repeats 51 M.V.S. at DROUVIN.	
			31/8/16 WNR	

War Diaries.

Major W R Rowston. A.V.C., A.D.V.S., 40th Division

Capt. G.B. Lancaster, A.V.C., O/c. 51st Mobile Vety Section

For month of
SEPTEMBER 1916.

WAR DIARY or INTELLIGENCE SUMMARY

MAJOR W.N. ROWSTON
A.D.V.S. - 40 Div

Army Form C. 2118
Vol 4

Place	Date	Hour	Summary of Events and Information	Remarks and references to Appendices
NOEUX	1/9/16		All V.O.s at office; weekly returns received, checked & consolidated return made out	
"	2/9/16		Weekly returns forwarded	
			Inspected animals of 121 Inf. Bde. Thus of 13 Regt, 20 Mules have bad condition and being pulled out. Transport officer of 113 Regt. complains of shortage of forage; advised to ensure more dust & water when on. An engagement in the absence of my pred. All injured horses evacuated 51 M.V.S.	
"	3/9/16		Attended conference of A.D.V.S. 1st Army at D.D.V.S. office at LILLERS	
			Visited 51 M.V.S. Inspected animals awaiting evacuation	
	4/9/16		Inspected animals of 120 Inf. Bde.; condition satisfactory on the whole; odd chres in 13 F Surrey not being hard, reported the to D.A.Q.M.G.	
	5/9/16		Sumalier Coen evacuated to 51 M.V.S.	

WAR DIARY
or
INTELLIGENCE SUMMARY

(Erase heading not required.)

Army Form C. 2118

Instructions regarding War Diaries and Intelligence Summaries are contained in F. S. Regs., Part II. and the Staff Manual respectively. Title Pages will be prepared in manuscript.

Place	Date	Hour	Summary of Events and Information	Remarks and references to Appendices
NOEUX	6/9/16		Infected animal of 40 Div R.E.; destruction on the whole strong; a number of spor have shown about evidence of a lack of grooming; van arrived w/3/ Convoy today sent to M.V.S. for evacuation. Infected another animal of F. Bde R.F.A. proceeded to transport. Under 51 M.V.S. & infected animal awaiting evacuation.	
	7/9/16		Office work & routine correspondence. All V.O's at office; mail return received & checked & completed.	
	8/9/16		Weekly return forwarded to D.D.V.S. Analysis animals evacuated to M.V.S.	
	9/9/16		Cut standing correspondence for the week cleared up.	
	10/9/16		Infected another animal 1 A.S.C., R.A. type transfer to Colonel H.T. Defrel. Infected than animal of 188 Bde R.F.A.; arranged for view of hired cobs.	

Army Form C. 2118

WAR DIARY
or
INTELLIGENCE SUMMARY
(Erase heading not required.)

Place	Date	Hour	Summary of Events and Information	Remarks and references to Appendices
NOEUX	11/9/16		Office work & correspondence. Impedimenta arrived in 51 M.V.S. awaiting evacuation.	
	12/9/16		Impedimenta arrived on arrival at NOEUX station & arranged distribution.	
	13/9/16		Impedimenta horses of 145 Bde R.F.A.; arranged for issue of horse cake to them in poor condition. Visited 51 M.V.S. & impedimenta same.	
	14/9/16		Impedimenta drawn of 181 Bde R.F.A. a very batch of them in very weak debilitated condition; arranged issue of horse cake. Egyptian animal evacuated to 51 M.V.S. A.D.V.O. at office; return received & checked & completed return compiled.	
	15/9/16		Impedimenta arrival of 119 9nf Bde; shown of Bde H.Q. made requisite attention; condition of animals good on the whole.	
	16/9/16		All impedimenta evacuation cleared up.	

Army Form C. 2118

WAR DIARY
or
INTELLIGENCE SUMMARY
(Erase heading not required.)

Place	Date	Hour	Summary of Events and Information	Remarks and references to Appendices
NOEUX	18/9/16		Inspected another horse of No R.A before then stamped to Renown Section at CONNEHEM; his hoof had a soft fore remove No 3 Section to Remn Park at HESDIGNEUL stable & then down for rest administration	
	19/9/16		Inspected animal of 120 2nd Bde; condition satisfactory. Seven animals wounded by S. MVS	
	20/9/16		Inspected remounts at NOEUX station. Inspected animals in S.MVS awaiting evacuation. Visited BETHUNE to see animals loaded into trains for hospital at St. OMER	
	22/9/16		Inspected animal of 121 2nd Bde; animal of 13 2nd & 20 Matthew showing line of condition other work satisfactory. All V.O.'s offer remounts returns received & checked & returns for the week made out	

WAR DIARY or INTELLIGENCE SUMMARY

Army Form C. 2118

Place	Date	Hour	Summary of Events and Information	Remarks and references to Appendices
NOEUX	23/9/16		Visited 51 MVS to inspect animals for evacuation. Trench an animal evacuated to 5. 51 MVS (13 belongs to 3rd Divsn)	
	24/9/16		Visited 51 MVS; horses & remounts drawn from Connehem & distributed to MVS	
	25/9/16		Visited A echelon 40 D.A.C. condition of animals good & things in good satisfactory. 178 & 258 T. Coy R.E. horsepower attached to 4th divn. V.O. & vet in ret charge	
	26/9/16		Visited B Echelon 40 D.A.C. condition of animals good & everything in good order & regard standing stables. Visited MVS & inspected animal under treatment	
	27/9/16		Officer went & inspected animal in MVS awaiting evacuation	

WAR DIARY
or
INTELLIGENCE SUMMARY

(Erase heading not required.)

Army Form C. 2118

Place	Date	Hour	Summary of Events and Information	Remarks and references to Appendices
NOEUX	25/9/15		Officer work	
			7 wounds cases evacuated to 51 M.V.S.	
	27/9/15		Inspected 2 centuries of No Div Train; condition of animals good, everything satisfactory	
			Inspected other two companies of 4o Div Train; condition of animals good & other things satisfactory.	
			All V.O's at office; returns for week made out	
	30/9/15		Weekly return forwarded to DDVS	
			All outstanding correspondence cleaned up.	
				W/N Rankine
				Major VS

WAR DIARY
INTELLIGENCE SUMMARY

Army Form C. 2118

ADVS 40 Div

Place	Date	Hour	Summary of Events and Information	Remarks and references to Appendices
NOEUX	1/10/16		Included arrivals of 121 9rd Bde & 127 9rd Pioneers. Arrival of unit in 12 gnd & 70 Middlesex when all ambulatory	
	2/10/16		Visited 51 MVS to inspect animals for evacuation. A very wet day	
	3/10/16		Office work. A very wet day. Twenty cases evacuated by 51 MVS	
	4/10/16		Visited 51 MVS to inspect animals for evacuation. Office work	
	5/10/16		Fourteen cases evacuated by 51 MVS	
	6/10/16		All V.O.s at office. return for the next week made out & quantity of clothing gone into & text return to prevent old days clothing being [illegible]	
	7/10/16		Weekly return dated due to ODOS 1st Army. Sixteen remounts drawn by 51MVS from [illegible]	

Army Form C. 2118

WAR DIARY
or
INTELLIGENCE SUMMARY
(Erase heading not required.)

Instructions regarding War Diaries and Intelligence Summaries are contained in F. S. Regs., Part II. and the Staff Manual respectively. Title Pages will be prepared in manuscript.

Place	Date	Hour	Summary of Events and Information	Remarks and references to Appendices
NOEUX	8/9/16		Attended conference at D.D.V.S. 1st Army Letter	
	9/9/16		Inspected horses of 178 Bde R.F.A.	
			" " " 120 Inf Bde	
	14/9/16		Inspected horses of 181 Bde R.F.A.	
			" " " 119 Inf Bde	
	16/9/16		Inspected horses of 158 Bde R.F.A.	
			Visited 51 M.V.S. & inspected 18 cases for evacuation	
	19/9/16		Proceeded on leave to England	
	22/9/16		Returned from leave "	
	21/9/16		Office work &c	
	22/9/16		Visited 51 M.V.S. & inspected cases for evacuation	
			Visits 121 Inf Bde	
			15 Cases evacuated to 51 M.V.S.	

WAR DIARY
or
INTELLIGENCE SUMMARY
(Erase heading not required.)

Army Form C. 2118

Place	Date	Hour	Summary of Events and Information	Remarks and references to Appendices
NOEUX	24/9/16		Officer work in morning. Visited 61 MVS to see cars for evacuation.	
	29/9/16		Drivers under orders to move (Len ambl?). Arranged to transfer Pte Rush from 181 Bn RFA to 119 Inf Bn on a temporary measure pte the orderly room the division.	
	30/9/16		Work return complete & despatches to DDMS 1st Army.	
ROLLE COURT	30/9/16		Officer work & getting things ready for move. Arrived at R Decourt.	
	31/9/16		Visited 51 MVS & inspected billets and horse lines.	

W Rawle

ADVS 40/25
WO X 6

WAR DIARY
or
INTELLIGENCE SUMMARY
(Erase heading not required.)

Army Form C. 2118

Place	Date	Hour	Summary of Events and Information	Remarks and references to Appendices
ROELLE-COURT	1/11/16		Visits D.D.V.S 3rd Army at St POL to enquire as to whom returns should be rendered and to make arrangements for collection of horses left en route.	
"	2/11/16		Visits 51 M.V.S billets in Ruellecourt. Officers & men in very bad. Weather extreme unsettled.	
"	3/11/16		With return complete & proceeded to 1st Army. Advanced Head Quarters moved to FROHEN-LE-GRAND	
FROHEN-LE GRAND			Advanced Head Quarters moved to BERNAVILLE. BERNAVILLE. Visit arrival to D.D.V.S 5 Army	
BERNAVILLE	4/11/16		Visits 51 M.V.S & inspects billets & clothing. Three field Companies of this division attached to 5 Army H.Q III Cake H.Qs & XIII Corps H.Q. Ambulances has weather told by 21 Mobileers & 13 Jork & arranged for unfit animals left behind to unfit ownership removed	
"	5/11/16		Visits HAUTE-VISEE & NEUVILLETTE to inspect animals left behind. Ambulances had meantime	

1875 Wt. W5893/826 1,000,000 4/15 J.B.C. & A. A.D.S.S./Forms/C. 2118.

Army Form C. 2118

WAR DIARY
or
INTELLIGENCE SUMMARY
(Erase heading not required.)

Place	Date	Hour	Summary of Events and Information	Remarks and references to Appendices
BERNAVILLE	8/11/16		Visited 119 Fd Amb H.Q. at AUTHEUX; 1m Field Regt at BOIS BERNARD; 18 Field at LE MEILLARD; No 26 ASC MoDu Train at LE MEILLARD; 12 Ind Regt (M) OUTREBOIS	
"	9/11/16		Visited HQ 120 Fd Amb H.G. at RIBEAUCOURT; 14 A.D.S. Highlander at same place; 11 Kmy Amn at PROUVILLE	
"	10/11/16		V.O. at Offices in morning with month return. Visited 13 MgnA ;21 Middlesex at CANDUS; 20 Middlesex at FIENVILLERS	
"	11/11/16		Month return completed & forwarded to DDVS 5th Army	
"	12/11/16		12 Fd Amb + 12 Ingd Provision & In 3 Fd Train left for 31 Dn. to be attached. Lieutenant. Morphia A.D.V.S. 31 Dn. Capt. De BOISSIERE A.S.C. in not change. Visited 12 Sufflh; 121 M. Gun Co at BERNEVIL	

Army Form C. 2118

WAR DIARY
or
INTELLIGENCE SUMMARY
(Erase heading not required.)

Instructions regarding War Diaries and Intelligence Summaries are contained in F.S. Regs., Part II. and the Staff Manual respectively. Title Pages will be prepared in manuscript.

Place	Date	Hour	Summary of Events and Information	Remarks and references to Appendices
BERNA-VILLE	13/4/16		Unpacked most of 119 Inf Bde; consolidation of animals gone on the whole.	
"	14/4/16		D.D.V.S. 5 Armn ranks division head quarters & other inspects 51 M.V.S.	
"	15/4/16		Moved to FROHEN-LE-GRAND, 51 M.V.S. billets in Ferme & Postal	
FROHEN-LE-GRAND	16/4/16		Inspected billets of 51 M.V.S. Five cases (Cav remount coy) evacuated to 51 M.V.S. Visited 18 Welsh & 19 R.W.F. Weekly return made out. Completed refunds on AVC accounts armature Office work.	
"	17/4/16		Moved to BOUQUEMAISON; 51 M.V.S. at ARBRES; inspected billets 5 Army of chance of area Visited 51 M.V.S. & inspected billets.	

WAR DIARY or INTELLIGENCE SUMMARY

Army Form C. 2118

(Erase heading not required.)

Place	Date	Hour	Summary of Events and Information	Remarks and references to Appendices
BOUQUE MAISON	20/11/16		Visited transport lines of 19th R.W.F. & 12th S.W.B. Went with D.A.D.O.S. to AMIENS to endeavour to purchase canvas for making meatsafes & to buy bayonets.	
"	21/11/16		Visited M.T. Co. A.S.C. Twelve cars examined by 51 M.V.S.	
"	22/11/16		From Thever to DOULLENS	
DOULLENS	23/11/16		Move to CANAPLES	
CANAPLES	24/11/16		Move to AILLY LE HAUT CLOCHER	
AILLY LE HAUT CLOCHER	25/11/16		Health return made out & forwarded to D.D.V.S. D.D.V.S. 5 Army; it drawn to new unit 5th Army. Standing order received from D.D.V.S. 5th Army.	

WAR DIARY
or
INTELLIGENCE SUMMARY
(Erase heading not required.)

Army Form C. 2118

Place	Date	Hour	Summary of Events and Information	Remarks and references to Appendices
AILLY LE H.CLOCHER	27/4/16		51 M.V.S. moved to new Outfall billets at FAMECHON. Units transport lines of 12 mgd Pioneers	
"	28/4/16		Office work	
"	29/4/16		On arrival visit O.C. No 2 Dr. Train, inspected all first line transport of 119 Inf. Bde. Inspected all first line transport of 120 Inf. Bde. Inspected animals for evacuation in 51 M.V.S. Thirty one animals drawn & used.	
"	30/4/16		Inspected all first line transport of 121 Inf. Bde. Nine animals evacuated to Abbeville & road & 51 M.V.S. Trades H.D. remounts drawn & used.	

WuR.

Army Form C. 2118

WAR DIARY
or
INTELLIGENCE SUMMARY

A.D.M.S. 40th Division

Vol 7

(Erase heading not required.)

Instructions regarding War Diaries and Intelligence Summaries are contained in F.S. Regs., Part II. and the Staff Manual respectively. Title Pages will be prepared in manuscript.

Place	Date	Hour	Summary of Events and Information	Remarks and references to Appendices
AILLY LE HAUT CLOCHER	1.12.16			
"	2/12/16		All WO's at Office. A.D.M.S. for the most checked and made out Infantries 17 gd (Premier) transport animals and 120 mules hym our transport animals. Visited 51 M.V.S.	
"	3/12/16		A new & other returns made out, forwarded to DDMS 4th Army. Infantries amounts of 229 Field Coy R.E. at Yaucourt. Infantries amounts of 134 Field Ambulance at Flixe. 224 Field Coy R.E. at Saen Riviere. Report made out & submitted to div. head quarters on all animals of front line transport of the division.	
"	4/12/16		Visited 51 M.V.S. & infantile animals for evacuation. Office work & routine correspondence.	
"	5/12/16		Infantries animals of 231 Field Coy R.E. at Buigny St Abbe. Ten cases evacuated by 51 M.V.S.	

Army Form C. 2118

WAR DIARY
or
INTELLIGENCE SUMMARY
(Erase heading not required.)

Place	Date	Hour	Summary of Events and Information	Remarks and references to Appendices
AILLY LE HAUCLOCHER	6/7/16		Orders received for move of Div to middle army XV Corps; transport & amount to go & there; personnel to go & there. Ten remount drawn from ABBEVILLE & distributed.	
	7/7/16		Visited 51 MVS; 3 Fd Ambs & RE & regtl Receiv left & drawn & to XV Div. V.O's at [?]; return received and checked	
	8/7/16		Transport 119 Inf Bde moved out. (St Riquier on ord change)	
	9/7/16		Waits return made out & despatched to D.D.V.S IV Army	
	10/7/16		Transport 121 Inf Bde moved out for new area. Ten carts ex rendr to 51 MVS	
	11/7/16		Nothing to record; orders our 2nd Ech move left until Div H.Q.	
	12/7/16		Nothing to record	
	13/7/16		Transport 120 Inf Bde & Div H.Q. and 51 MVS started for new area	
	14/7/16			
	15/7/16		Posted up offices advances; nothing to record.	

WAR DIARY or INTELLIGENCE SUMMARY

Army Form C. 2118

Place	Date	Hour	Summary of Events and Information	Remarks and references to Appendices
AILLY LE H.C.	15/12/16		Moved from AILLY LE HAUT CLOCHER to CHIPILLY the division taking over billets & camps in that area from French Army. Nothing of interest in CHIPILLY. 51 MVS billets in CHIPILLY all V.G. as office.	
CHIPILLY	16/12/16		Visited 119 Inf Bde bivouac in Camp 12. About half the command under cover in wooden abilities [huts] left by the French, no made standing over even in huts. Divn have been three days in transit, the open as bedding shelters. Their units not known in the open as bedding shelters.	
"	17/12/16		Visited 121 Inf Bde bivouac in Camp 12 & 12A. I am shown shelters in Camp 12A & turn shelter in Gottschen in open lines & standing in mud. Up till the units were now in SAILLY LAURETTE & Camp 12. The men standing ankle in mud in approaches made to an of the accommodation for their men.	
"	18/12/16		Visited 120 Inf Bde bivouac in Camp 11/12/12. All huron in [?] often [?] in high ground sift must not in [?] by or by the often camps. Weather fr frost – three days new cold would spoil.	

WAR DIARY
INTELLIGENCE SUMMARY

Army Form C. 2118

Place	Date	Hour	Summary of Events and Information	Remarks and references to Appendices
CHIPILLY	20/12/16		Visited Advanced lines of 11 Hors Gds Lancers & 14 H.L.9 at Camp 13	
	21/12/16		The amounts under own for inactive stables but so much as approach ponds to shew how horses are unpossible to push to keep the animals dry, clean or dry.	
			Seven can reported to 51 M.V.S.	
			Inc. comm. to show animals and stopt have cleaning a few cases of contained mather have occurred due to its exposure old weather & nervousness of the horses but shutting in but most situation were received — studied	
			All V.O.'s at office the morning, stores received — studied	
	22/12/16			
	23/12/16		Attended conference at IV Army Head quarters	
	24/12/16		Visited advanced lines of 119 Inf Bde.	
	25/12/16		Xmas day; no work had to meets	
	26/12/16		51 M.V.S. gone to billets in new area at BRAY.	
			Inspected billets of many M.V.S. at BRAY.	
	27/12/16		The drawn commences to move to forward area in relief of 33 Dn	
			Seven cases evacuated to 51 M.V.S.	

WAR DIARY
or
INTELLIGENCE SUMMARY

(Erase heading not required.)

Army Form C. 2118

Place	Date	Hour	Summary of Events and Information	Remarks and references to Appendices
CHIPILLY	28/11/18		Dn H.Q. move from Chipilly ; Dn H.Q. Echelon B to stay on at L.16.d.1.9 (ALBERT continued about) H.Qrs Adv. H.Q. & B 21.c. on new about	
L.16.d.1.9 (BRAY)	29/11		All V.O's at office with returns ; Units 51 MVS completed cars for evacuation	
"	30/11		Under range lines of 198 Bde R.F.A. evacuation of horse spent ; all under one of parts but evacuation to area of deep mud & trench to plantin with mud. Trench care divided by 51 MVS ; one car of many, in H.Q. G. 40 Dn. When the animal has been detached with 33rd Dn.	
"	1/12/18		Under 134 Heavy Bty (XV Co Artillery) to enemy for character of shells; trough means to outbreak of cant-again domestice ; information DDVS & Corn of other Wigham.	

W.N.R.

WAR DIARY
or
INTELLIGENCE SUMMARY

(Erase heading not required.)

Army Form C. 2118

ADVS 40 DN

Vol 8

Place	Date	Hour	Summary of Events and Information	Remarks and references to Appendices
Lt d 1.9 Abt when start from m BR 159	1.1.19		Ordered 51 MVS to inspect 25 animals for evacuation; mostly debility. Remainder sympathetic wound noon to sit. duel mud in and in the avenues them to work slower in on the avenues	
"	2.1.19		Visited transport lines of 1/19 Inf Bde near MAUREPAS lines very bad & muddy & no road to them; animals our meridiem than condition 4 mules evacuated to 51 MVS	
"	3.1.19		Infantile animals of 1 Bg & DAC ; When animals are keeping their condition fairly well lines on and animals to deep mud & in poor shape. A mule evacuated to 51 MVS.	
"	4.1.19		Visited 124 Hy Bty lines (X Corps H.A.G.) at MAUREPAS animals in into a sea of entragene dimenible; immediate report to DDVS IV Army Ten cases evacuated to 51 MVS	
"	5.1.19		AV VO at Afrt Return nones Studies Visited 51 MVS to inspect 9 cases for evacuation	

Army Form C. 2118

WAR DIARY
or
INTELLIGENCE SUMMARY
(Erase heading not required.)

Instructions regarding War Diaries and Intelligence Summaries are contained in F. S. Regs, Part II. and the Staff Manual respectively. Title Pages will be prepared in manuscript.

Place	Date	Hour	Summary of Events and Information	Remarks and references to Appendices
4. (?) ig in BRAY	6.11.19		Attended conference at D.D.V.S. office 4 Army H.Q. Two cases of contagious dermatitis admitted to No 3 Sectn 40 DAC, sent with return to V.O. i/c; autopsy DDVS – Dn H.Q. 8 cases evacuated to 51 MVS	
	7/11/19		Inspected horses of J/B Bde R.F.A.; the animal infection show of B Battery been fallen M to great deal whilst in infantry, but appeared convalescent. a number of mud o horsemen (left by the French). 21 cases evacuated to 51 MVS.	
	8/11/19		Visited 21 W Irish Dragoons (attached from III Div) to inspect infected animals seen 9 animals with skin complaint. advised them to evacuate infected animal to 1/20 Ind Bde, 1/22 R.E. 729 R.E. at MAUREPAS no more horses, thought they were to 9/229 R.E of DAGNY & No6 Div. Forwarded infected horse down to DAGNY & no Div 16 cases evacuated to 51 MVS	
	9/11/19		Visited 51 MVS to inspect cases for evacuation. Infantile hospital Command of Lt. Stone full. Ambulances at SUZANNE evacuated to 51 MVS	

WAR DIARY or INTELLIGENCE SUMMARY

Army Form C. 2118

Place	Date	Hour	Summary of Events and Information	Remarks and references to Appendices
Nr BRAY	10/11/19		Visited M.V.S. to inspect cases for evacuation. Officers orderlies &c. 38 animals evacuated by 51 MVS	
"	11/11/19		Visited MVS to inspect 25 cases for evacuation. Inspected animals of units of 121 M Bde at Suzanne	
"	12/11/19		All V.O.'s at office, returns received & checked. Visited MVS to inspect 30 cases for evacuation.	
"	13/11/19		Visited no Dn G.C. to inspect animals suffering from conjunc. stomatitis, 10 to inspect arrangement for isolation of animals suffering therefrom; affected cases sent to isolation lines at ETINEHEM	
"	14/11/19		Visited MVS to inspect 36 cases for evacuation	
"	15/11/19		Visited Dn & Section 33 DAC to inspect case of atomatitis. Made arrangements for isolation & modern isolation of the unit. Sent report to DDVS. 15 left K.G. 19 animals for evacuation. Visited 51 MVS & inspected	

WAR DIARY
or
INTELLIGENCE SUMMARY

Army Form C. 2118

Place	Date	Hour	Summary of Events and Information	Remarks and references to Appendices
# BRAY	16/11/17		Infantry ammunition of 181 Bde R.F.A: all other ammunition being constantly replenished went to hand and 2 ground test condition. Met 2 detachments 68 ammunition to infantry, R.E., A.S.C. mounts. 19 ammunition wounded to 51 M.V.S.	
	17/11/17		Under 11 m H.A. very urgent horse & case evacuated by 51 M.V.S	
	18/11/17		Office routine.	
	19/11/17		All V.O's at office. Under Dm Sutton 33 DAC to inspect ammunition under veterinary subaltern almostho. 14 Case evacuated to 51 MVS	
	20/11/17		Attended conference at D.D.V.S. 4 Corps H.Q. 16 Case evacuated to 51 MVS.	

WAR DIARY
or
INTELLIGENCE SUMMARY

Army Form C. 2118

(Erase heading not required.)

Instructions regarding War Diaries and Intelligence Summaries are contained in F. S. Regs., Part II. and the Staff Manual respectively. Title Pages will be prepared in manuscript.

Place	Date	Hour	Summary of Events and Information	Remarks and references to Appendices
Nr BRAY	21/11/19		Impulse arrival of 1yf Bde R.F.A. i ammunit on tram ambulance lorries to grand teams frozen hard there is been needs dermateter. Under No DHC to be no impulse case of climate. Under 14 Cases evacuated to 51 MVS	
	22/11/19		Under 137 Heavy Bde wagon lines to be no impulse many cases auxiliary return. Under 229 R.E. lines to report feeding arrangements. 8 cases evacuated to 51 MVS.	
	23/11/19		Under 51 MVS to report 39 cases for evacuation	
	24/11/19		Under transport lines of 13 Bgd. o 12 Buffs at SUZANNE	
	25/11/19		Under 51 MVS. 9 cases evacuated to 51 MVS	

WAR DIARY
or
INTELLIGENCE SUMMARY
(Erase heading not required.)

Army Form C. 2118

Place	Date	Hour	Summary of Events and Information	Remarks and references to Appendices
Nr BRAY	26/11/19		All V.O's at Offrs Mess. return received & checked. Visited 51 MVS	
	27/11/19		Visited 51 MVS to inspect animals under treatment (40 in number) All convalescent horsepower conducted move to readway congestion	
	28/11/19		Drove in western & R.E. mass but to middle area; Dn H.G. & CORBIE 51 MVS to CHIPILLY	
	29/11/19		Opened Offrs at Ends Mabinall CORBIE Inspected horsepower amount of 120 mf Bde in & around CORBIE	
	30/11/19		Attended conference at D.D.V.S. 13 Army.	
	31/11/19		Drove by that present while Gun. Ln. here in the line. 51 animals have been thoroughly thru the MVS. I ther 125 men received at the odw; collection station at MARICOURT; 466 have been evacuated, 5 died & destroyed; 14 returned to work; 15 handed over to advance MVS; 143 returned to treatment. Strength I can ascertain, considers dermatitis; scurvy mostly & continues but has been confirmed.	
				W.W.R.

WAR DIARY
or
INTELLIGENCE SUMMARY

Army Form C. 2118

ADVS 40D

SD9

Place	Date	Hour	Summary of Events and Information	Remarks and references to Appendices
CORBIE	1/2/19		Visited 51 MVS at Chipilly to inspect animals under treatment suffering from no mange.	
"	2/2/19		Inspected animals of 119 M Gun Coy at Camp 12; then went about many 0 o not many horses infected and sent to A.D.S. M.L. incurrun stam. Two cases animals syphilis in No 2 Salvn Mo DAC. All V O o of Mhm; relium received & checked	
"	3/2/19		Visited No 36 ASC to inspect animal until other draws (found to be fairly mangy or mumpine examination. Visited 120 M.B.G. & 13 t Survey Infantes Gen can animals in 149 Rd RFA; horses in 181 Bde RFA, horses in 23 Field Co RE. Infants transport animals 911 R2O Royal Corps.	
"	4/2/19		Office routine	
"	5/2/19		There were animals in 149 Bde RFA; one in B 181 Bde RFA	
"	6/2/19		Visited 51 MVS at Chipilly & Inspected of 119 2t Bde at Camp 12 >13 at Chipilly. Gun can animals in B181 RFA; 3 cases in 40 DAC	

WAR DIARY
or
INTELLIGENCE SUMMARY

Army Form C. 2118

Place	Date	Hour	Summary of Events and Information	Remarks and references to Appendices
CORBIE	7/9/19		Units 19[?]Bd. R.F.A. morgn[?] from at Camp 20 men Suzanne to see what provision men see been taken with regard to ambulance cases.	
"	8/9/19		I no horse cases in D19F R.F.A. Officer reading [illegible]	
"	9/9/19		All V.O. at office with return. 1 no case admitted in B181 R.F.A.	
"	10/9/19		Units S.A. Sehr no DAC at Vaux are ambulant abuvable case from to march for myris. Units 51 MUS at Chipilly no arrangs for caring men of the redire	
"	11/9/19		Officer rendin[?] ; packed up office but ready to move on 12th.	

WAR DIARY
or
INTELLIGENCE SUMMARY

(Erase heading not required.)

Army Form C. 2118

Place	Date	Hour	Summary of Events and Information	Remarks and references to Appendices
CORBIE	10/9/19		Div H.Q. move from CORBIE ; Col. H.Q. to MAUREPAS. Recce H.Q. to dig nits at L.6 d.1.9 (Albert Cardonnet Rd.) near BRAY. 51 MVS move to BRAY VILLERS. Visits 51 MVS & inspects billets.	
Nr BRAY	13/9/19		Visits Dy 4 R.A.S.C & ETINEHEM to inspect arrangements for drainage; ten cases put to get back to work. 1 on dan admitted to B.181 B.d R.F.A. 46 cases evacuated to 51 MVS.	
"	14/9/19		Attends conference 1 DDVS IV Corps at IV Corps H.Q. One can admitted to B.181 R.F.A; one in D/4 R.F.A. Inspects horses of 181 Bd R.F.A; all animals in firm condition.	
"	15/9/19		All V.O's at office ; return received & checked. The scheme examined.	

WAR DIARY
or
INTELLIGENCE SUMMARY

(Erase heading not required.)

Army Form C. 2118

Instructions regarding War Diaries and Intelligence Summaries are contained in F. S. Regs., Part II. and the Staff Manual respectively. Title Pages will be prepared in manuscript.

Place	Date	Hour	Summary of Events and Information	Remarks and references to Appendices
In BRAY	18/4/19		Inspected animals of 178 Bde R.F.A.; in fair condition but some leg eczema. One case strangles in B/8¹ R.F.A.; one dun in D/178	
"	19/4/19		An interview with O.C. Div Train inspected 1st line transport of 12 Suffolks. 2.0 Mulleins S/21 M.G. Coy. One case strangles in C/8¹ R.F.A.	
"	20/4/19		An interview with O.C. Div Train inspected 1st line transport of 21 Mulleins 113th Bde; site latrine in poor condition. Ten cases strangles in B/8¹ R.F.A. Units & D.A.C. to inspect animals cases of strangles, fumes to be fully clean & dis-infecting only. One case strangles in H.Q./8¹ R.F.A.; one in D/178 R.F.A. Ten - four cases evacuated to 51 M.V.S.	
"	21/4/19		Units 18 Bde R.F.A. MVS in B/8¹ R.F.A. One case strangles in B/8¹ R.F.A.	

WAR DIARY or INTELLIGENCE SUMMARY

Army Form C. 2118

(Erase heading not required.)

Place	Date	Hour	Summary of Events and Information	Remarks and references to Appendices
Nr BRAY	22/9/17		Visit O.C. Dns Trains infantry 14" H.L.I. 51st D. & S. Hyh. 120 M.G. Coy. 1st Line Transport	
"	23/9/17		One Car attended in B.S.S. RFA. All V.O's at office with return. Unit's S.M.V.S. to inspect animals for evacuation	
"	24/9/17		Office routine &c	
"	25/9/17		Visits to R.A.S.C. &c infant. 19 evac. animals came from 40 Div. Trysth visit O.C. Dn Train infantry 1st Line Transport of 120 M.G. Coy. Submits report to Dn H.Q.	
"	26/9/17		Ordrs issued for V-Officer ser VO 40 D.A.C. to proceed to 2/15 A.H.A.S. for duty. Office	
"	26/9/17		Attended conference at D.D.V.S. IV Army	

W.W. Rynache
Major V.V.
26/9/17

A.D.V.S 4th Div [signature]
Army Form C. 2118

WAR DIARY
or
INTELLIGENCE SUMMARY
(Erase heading not required.)

Place	Date	Hour	Summary of Events and Information	Remarks and references to Appendices
BRAY	1.3.19		Inspected in conjunction with O.C. Train Ford line transport of 1/4.R.W.F. Walsh & 119 M.G. Coy (119 Inf Bd) Visited 51 M.V.S. & inspect animals under treatment awaiting evacuation	
"	2.3.19		In conjunction with O.C. Train inspected first line transport of 1/19 R.W.F. & 12th S.W.B. (119 Inf Bd) Submitted report on the Casualties to the animals of these units under command to Div. H.Q. All V.C. off. officers with whom ac—	
"	3.3.19		Visited 51 M.V.S. to inspect animals under treatment & convalescent. Weather returns required, but— 21 cases evacuated to 51 M.V.S. Visited SUZANNE to arrange billets for M.V.S.	
"	4.3.19		Office matters	
"	5.3.19		Inspected animals of 1st Bn. R.F.A. 34 cases evacuated to 51 M.V.S.	
"	6.3.19		Visited 51 M.V.S.	

WAR DIARY
or
INTELLIGENCE SUMMARY
(Erase heading not required.)

Army Form C. 2118

Place	Date	Hour	Summary of Events and Information	Remarks and references to Appendices
BRAY	8.3.19		Recd H.Q. under orders to move to SUZANNE in the 9th inst, packed up stores in readiness	
SUZANNE	9.3.19		Moved to Suzanne; Offrs in shelters; 51/MVS in billets in the village. O.C. VG- & Offrs in the Minimum	
"	10.3.19		Under no Du T care at BRAY. Return to the unit made out & forwarded. 28 Cases evacuated to 51/MVS	
"	11.3.19		Under no 4 Recce Pool at ETINEHEM to inspect animals in their respective units prior to their return to these respective units	
"	12.3.19		Went round transport lines of all units of 1149 M Bde at FRISE. Under 51/MVS & inspected men and horses & sleeping accommodation	

WAR DIARY or INTELLIGENCE SUMMARY

Army Form C. 2118

Place	Date	Hour	Summary of Events and Information	Remarks and references to Appendices
SUZANNE	13/3/19		Visited 137 H.B. (It Col H.A.L.) to instruct him & inform to left behind on the move of the unit to another area	
"	14/3/19		Visited details of 20 Brigade, 12 Supply Col. 121 M.G. Cy at Camp 19 (Suzanne). Syphilis cases evacuated to 51 M.D.S. Office routine	
"	15/3/19		Visited to M.O. i/c Dn Train at Bray to question case of foot treatment & a gunshot case. Stimson spent in unknown ways receiving all V.O.'s at office	
"	16/3/19			
"	17/3/19		Visited branches Ammn of 224, 231, 229 Field Coys R.E. & 12 York Regmn of TRIBE & HEM Wrote return arising out of personnel 32 Cases evacuated to 51 M.D.S. Office routine	
"	18/3/19			

Army Form C. 2118

WAR DIARY
or
INTELLIGENCE SUMMARY
(Erase heading not required.)

Place	Date	Hour	Summary of Events and Information	Remarks and references to Appendices
SUZANNE	19.3.17		Infants arrived 181 Bde RFA; a pm lt until new amount between in details. Infants arrived in 51 MDS awaiting evacuation	
"	20/3/17		51 Can wounded to 51 MUS	
"	21/3/17		Dr H.Q. B Eccles moved to CURLU; my offrs moved to P.C. Jean & Curlu; arrange for 51 MUS to move to Curlu also	
CURLU	22.3.17		Ypres offrs at P.C. Jean	
"	23/3/17		All U.G. at offrs' returns received checked	
"	24/3/17		Verdun Newport line of 121 Inf Bde at HAUT ALLAINE & MT. ST QUENTIN. H.Q. De Treem & FRISE	
"	25/3/17		"	
"	26/3/17		Infants arrived in 51 MUS awaiting evacuation	
"	27/3/17		Moved offrs to P.C. CRANIERE near MAUREPAS (B.g.g.s.f Albert Cambrai Rue)	

WAR DIARY
or
INTELLIGENCE SUMMARY

(Erase heading not required.)

Army Form C. 2118

Place	Date	Hour	Summary of Events and Information	Remarks and references to Appendices
Pt. CRANIERE	28/3/19		Ampleflex arrived under lieutenant [illegible] according to orders in 51 MUS	
"	29/3/19		Office work	
"	30/3/19		All W.O.'s & Offrs & mens return received & checked	
"	31/3/19		In conform with O.C. Dn Train made an inspection of 14 MG, 14 AS, Hydrasters & 120 MG (120 mg B.C.) at FRISE-BEND all found [illegible] in reasonable amounts.	

W Routin
Major RAMC
ADMS GOPu

31/3/19

ON HIS MAJESTY'S SERVICE.

Confidential

War Diary
of
Major W. H. Rowston. A.V.C.
A.D.V.S. 40th Division.
from 1/4/17 to 30/4/17.

Army Form C. 2118

WAR DIARY
or
INTELLIGENCE SUMMARY ARTV S 402
(Erase heading not required.)

Place	Date	Hour	Summary of Events and Information	Remarks and references to Appendices
P.C. CRANIERE (MAUREPAS)	1/4/19		Infantry 11 Hampton line & 13 E Surrey Regiments Newport and O.C. Du Train.	
"	2/4/19		Under 51 MVS at CURLU to report of 1 no 9 Pdr to Div HQ. Lore motion. Forwarded report in Newport of 1 no 9 Pdr to Div HQ.	
"	3/4/19		Under Newport line of 1, 1 91 Inf Bde at MONT ST QUENTIN to investigate report that ammts now drying from however. Carr of shell found to be exhaustion & exfreme patro. Infantry Newport ammts of 119 & 2nd Inf Bde together with O.C Du Train all the ammts have fallen in off in condition owing to long march & test march the condition, what return & from ammts being under strength in ammts & whether not possible the next army of them	
"	4/4/19		Офри routine	

1875 Wt. W593/826 1,000,000 4/15 J.B.C. & A. A.D.S.S./Forms/C. 2118.

WAR DIARY
or
INTELLIGENCE SUMMARY
(Erase heading not required.)

Army Form C. 2118

Place	Date	Hour	Summary of Events and Information	Remarks and references to Appendices
P.C. CRANIERE	5/4/19		Visited 51 MVS at CURLU to inspect animals under treatment awaiting evacuation	
"	6/4/19		All O.C.'s at office with returns	
"	7/4/19		During the preceding week the mortality among the animals has been high owing to hard work, bad weather & exposure ; 145 animals have been discharged for debility & exhaustion ; the 33 have died from the same cause ; nearly all other animals are in P.P. units & have been marked unfit ; they num[ber] ??? & casting shells on very bad roads ; ration has been short for the animals, they have had no wheelen [woollen?] a nunat [?] fodder, compound for which is not had there.	
"	8.4.19		Visited 51 MVS in its new field at MOISLAINS; great accumulation in	
"	9.4.19		Office routine	

Army Form C. 2118

WAR DIARY
or
INTELLIGENCE SUMMARY
(Erase heading not required.)

Instructions regarding War Diaries and Intelligence Summaries are contained in F.S. Regs., Part II. and the Staff Manual respectively. Title Pages will be prepared in manuscript.

Place	Date	Hour	Summary of Events and Information	Remarks and references to Appendices
P.C. MAHIERE	10.4.17		In company with O.C. Du Train inspected 1st line transport of 121 Inf Bde at MANANCOURT & ETRICOURT. All animals shewn fettles off in condition result of hard work exposure & shortage of numerals rations. 44 can evacuated by 51 MVS	
"	11.4.17		Office; went in 2 I Rd animals evacuated to Dr H Q.	
"	12.4.17		Inspected animals of 1/51 Bde RFA at MANANCOURT. This unit is much under strength in animals & the remounts are in poor condition	
"	13.4.17		All V.O.'s of office visits return &c.	
MANANCOURT	14.4.17		Shewed office at MANANCOURT (Sheet 57C i V13)	
"	15.4.17		Inspected animals of No Du Train at MOISLAINS (Mules in the whole good)	

WAR DIARY or INTELLIGENCE SUMMARY

Army Form C. 2118

Place	Date	Hour	Summary of Events and Information	Remarks and references to Appendices
MANANCOURT	16/4/17		Inspected A, B & D Btys, 1st Bde R.F.A. arrived at EQUANCOURT. Conditions moderate on the whole. Inspected wounds awaiting evacuation in 51 MVS	
"	17/4/17		Inspected wounds of C/178 Bde R.F.A. at ETRICOURT, in rather poor condition. 29 wounds evacuated to 51 MVS	
"	18/4/17		Visited 178th Bde R.F.A. to inspect animals, replies to be compared to schedule; arranged for weekly test.	
"	19/4/17		Visited 51 MVS to inspect animals under treatment	
"	20/4/17		All V.Os at HQ 51 MVS re inspect animals for evacuation	
"	21/4/17		Inspected animals 1 & 81 Bde R.F.A. Sixteen cases evacuated to 51 MVS	

WAR DIARY or INTELLIGENCE SUMMARY

Army Form C. 2118

Place	Date	Hour	Summary of Events and Information	Remarks and references to Appendices
MANANCOURT	22/4/19		Ampulets arrived of B. Echelon 40th D.A.C. at CLERY	
"	23/4/19		Ampulets arrived 1 M.1 & 2 Sections 40th D.A.C. Visited 51 M.V.S. obt. input arrived for evacuation	
"	24/4/19		Ampulets arrived of 231 Field R.E. at ETRICOURT. Trench cars unmetalled to 51 M.V.S.	
"	25/4/19		Orders received from DD to Cpt to form a rest station for horses arranges to form one at MOISLAINS under supervision of 51 M.V.S. Arranged for tent, forage, rations, mobile troughs to be put up + load of bedding of 51 M.V.S. not opened; also field cable by	
"	26/4/19		Ampulets arrived of D.51. R.F.A. proven to Span at IV Army Baths	
"	27/4/19		Office	

WAR DIARY
or
INTELLIGENCE SUMMARY

(Erase heading not required.)

Army Form C. 2118

Place	Date	Hour	Summary of Events and Information	Remarks and references to Appendices
MANANCOURT	28/4/19		Impales amount of 120 2nd Bde > packed out amounts of red Camp. Under 51 MUS > red camp.	
	29/4/19		Under 298 Bde RFA at CERISY to unpack 168 down hung tents over to 40 Dn R.D.	
	30/4/19		Impales amount of 119 2nd Bde at FINS > packed out amounts for the red camp.	WHR.

War Diary of Major. W. N. Rowston. A.V.C.
A.D.V.S. 40th Division. May 1/31st 1917.

War Diary of Capt. G.C. Lancaster. A.V.C.
O.C. 51st Mobile Vety Section. May 1/31st 1917.

WAR DIARY
or
INTELLIGENCE SUMMARY.

(Erase heading not required.)

Place	Date	Hour	Summary of Events and Information	Remarks and references to Appendices
MANANCOURT	1.5.19		Inspected ammunition of 121 9rd Bde at ETRICOURT & picked out ammunition for not camp	
"	2.5.19		Visited 40 Dn Train at MOISLAINS to inspect ammunition to refunds & RE units	
			Visited 181 Bde RFA to inspect at EGUANCOURT to inspect his ammunition case of damage, also 50 rounds being sent to IV Army School	
"	3.5.19		Attended D.D.V.S. Conference at IV Army H.Q at VILLERS-CARBONVEL	
			All V.O's at office, returns received & checked	
			Visited 51 MVS to inspect ammunition in rest station	
"	4.5.19		Visited 155 Heavy Bty Wagon lines at EGUANCOURT to inspect wagons Inspected ammunition of Jn8 Bde RFA in an evacuated bn 51 MVS	
"	6.5.19		Officer Met Dn Gun Officer to try and see how ammunition and average ammunition in the bn for all units of the division	

WAR DIARY
or
INTELLIGENCE SUMMARY.

(Erase heading not required.)

Army Form C. 2118.

Place	Date	Hour	Summary of Events and Information	Remarks and references to Appendices
MANANCOURT	7.5.19		Visited 155 Hvy Bty at EQUANCOURT to inspect many cases	
			Visited 51 MVS to inspect animals for evacuation	
"	8.5.19		Office	
			To meet our cases evacuated by 51 MVS	
"	9.5.19		Visited 40 Div Train at ncernur. Saw anipulid cases of mange	
"	10.5.19		Visited 9th H.A.G. Head Quarto at FINS re outbreak of mange in 155 Hy Bty	
			Office. all V.O.s of offices with return re	
"	11/5/19		Visited 51 MVS to inspect animals for evacuation	
"	12.5.19		Office	
			on cases evacuated by 51 MVS	

WAR DIARY
or
INTELLIGENCE SUMMARY.
(Erase heading not required.)

Army Form C. 2118.

Place	Date	Hour	Summary of Events and Information	Remarks and references to Appendices
MANANCOURT	13.5.19		Met DDVS IV Army at MOISLAINS who inspected 51.MVS; arranged in the Horse Rest Station at MOISLAINS & arranged of 155 Hvy Bde & part of 178 Bde RFA at EQUANCOURT	
"	14.5.19		Inspected transport arranged of 119 Inf Bde at FINS & submitted report to DnH.G. Inspected horse & evacuation in 51 MVS	
"	15/5/19		Visited M & G.O Du Train to examine mysseline mange cases. Twenty cases evacuated to 51 MVS	
"	16/5/19		Office routine	
"	17/5/19		Visited 51.MVS & inspected animals arrived in the rest station	
"	18/5/19		All V.O.s at offices inspected animals for evacuation in 51 MVS	

Army Form C. 2118.

WAR DIARY
or
INTELLIGENCE SUMMARY.

(Erase heading not required.)

Place	Date	Hour	Summary of Events and Information	Remarks and references to Appendices
MANANCOURT	19.5.19		Office routine	
"	20.5.19		Thirties cases evacuated to 51 M.V.S.	
			Office & admin routine	
"	21.5.19		In conform with O.C. Du Toun infantes all post line hospital 12.0.3.12.1 Maj Bohm; a canditete all round improvement in the animals since recent arrival & prepare become available. Unites 51 M.V.S. to inspect animals for evacuation & rating horses	
"	22.5.19		Admany routine	
			8 cases evacuated to 51 M.V.S	
"	23.5.19		Admany routine	

Instructions regarding War Diaries and Intelligence Summaries are contained in F. S. Regs., Part II. and the Staff Manual respectively. Title pages will be prepared in manuscript.

Army Form C. 2118.

WAR DIARY
or
INTELLIGENCE SUMMARY.
(Erase heading not required)

Instructions regarding War Diaries and Intelligence Summaries are contained in F. S. Regs., Part II. and the Staff Manual respectively. Title pages will be prepared in manuscript.

Place	Date	Hour	Summary of Events and Information	Remarks and references to Appendices
MANANCOURT	24/5/17		CO & O's at office. Visited 135 Field Ambulance at MARICOURT & inspected transport arrangts	
"	25/5/17		All V.O.s at office. Inspected returns & returns	
"	26/5/17		Adminy routine	
"	27/5/17		Inspected arrangts of 229, 224, 231 Field Coys R.E. at FINS & SOREL. Also arrangts of 1st Gds Pioneers at FINS.	
"	28/5/17		Visited No 1 Gds ASC at MANANCOURT & inspected arrangts & many cases	
"	29/5/17		Adminy routine	
"	30/5/17		Inspected horse lines No 4 D.A.C. horses. & arranged re artillery med. card	
"	31/5/17		Adminy routine	

W.N. Roche
Major
ADMS

Army Form C. 2118.

WAR DIARY
or
INTELLIGENCE SUMMARY.

(Erase heading not required.)

ADVS 40 Div

Place	Date	Hour	Summary of Events and Information	Remarks and references to Appendices
MANANCOURT	1.6.19		All V.O's at office with return &c. Ampulles cannot be dis-infected & animals for evacuation in S.I M.V.S	
"	2.6.19		Return & office routine. Three cases evacuated to S.I M.V.S	
"	3.6.19		Afternoon routine	
"	4.6.19		Afternoon routine	
"	5.6.19		Ampulles arrived 1/181 Bde R.F.A. i/c cavalcade improvement all round	
"	6.6.19		Ampulles arrived 1 B. Soldier 40th D.A.C.; all in good condition	
"	7.6.19		Ampulles arrived 1 No. Section 40 D.A.C.; condition very good	
"	8.6.19		Attended horse for the relation of ante pro & horse first in III Cdn. Area; ante relation near ETRICOURT. All V.O's at office with return	

Army Form C. 2118.

WAR DIARY
or
INTELLIGENCE SUMMARY.
(Erase heading not required)

Instructions regarding War Diaries and Intelligence Summaries are contained in F. S. Regs., Part II. and the Staff Manual respectively. Title pages will be prepared in manuscript.

Place	Date	Hour	Summary of Events and Information	Remarks and references to Appendices
MANANCOURT	9.6.19		Gunnery routine	
"	10.6.19		Truck cars rendezvous by 51 MVS	
			Gunnery routine	
"	11.6.19		Gunnery routine	
"	12.6.19		Gave lecture on Horsemastership in the Field at IV Army Artillery School at VAUX en AMIENOIS	
			Five cars rendezvous by 51 MVS	
"	13.6.19		Gunnery routine	
"	14.6.19		Gunnery routine	
			2 pack animals of 148 Bde RFA condition good on the whole	
			All V.O.'s at office with return	
"	15.6.19		Ampules amount for rendezvous in 51 MVS	
			Ampules transport animals of 120 2nd Bde condition good on the whole	
"	16.6.19		Truck cars rendezvous by 51 MVS	

(A7092). Wt W12859/M1293. 75,000. 1/17. D D. & L., Ltd. Forms/C.2118/14.

Army Form C. 2118.

WAR DIARY
or
INTELLIGENCE SUMMARY.
(Erase heading not required.)

Instructions regarding War Diaries and Intelligence Summaries are contained in F. S. Regs., Part II. and the Staff Manual respectively. Title pages will be prepared in manuscript.

Place	Date	Hour	Summary of Events and Information	Remarks and references to Appendices
MANANCOURT	17.6.17		Amputees transport arrived of 121 Inf Bde Transport - condition good on the whole	
"	18.6.17		Amputees transport arrived of 119 Inf Bde ; condition good German nature. 8 cars inverted by 51 MVS.	
"	19.6.17		"	
"	20.6.17		Amputees arrived of 40th Sqnd Co.	
"	21.6.17		Amputees arrived in MVS & met station	
"	22.6.17		All V.C. at office and return Amputees arrived for evacuation in 51 MVS	
"	23.6.17		Amputees arrived of Div A.S. Hyflenden & 13 E. Survey German cars evacuated by 51 MVS	
"	24.6.17			
"	25.6.17		Proceeded on 10 day leave.	

WNR Major ADVS
DADVS 40th Division

War Diary of DADVS, 40th Divn
July 1st 1917

War Diary of O.C. 51st M.V.S.
July 1st 1917

Army Form C. 2118.

WAR DIARY
or
INTELLIGENCE SUMMARY. 40 Div. D.A.D.V.S.

(Erase heading not required.)

Vol 14

Place	Date	Hour	Summary of Events and Information	Remarks and references to Appendices
MANANCOURT	7.7.19		Returned from leave	
"	8.7.19		Office routine	
"	9.7.19		Impulses arrived in 51 MVS	
"	10.7.19		Office routine	
"			Twenty one cases evacuated to 51 MVS	
"	11.7.19		Office moved to SOREL-LE-GRAND. (V.18.d.5.7 Sheet 57c)	
SOREL	12.7.19		Impulses arrived of 181 Bde R.F.A.	
"	13.7.19		All V.O's at office return re sick	
			Under MVS + impulses arrived for evacuation	
			Impulses arrived of D/178 Bde R.F.A.	
"	14.7.19		Impulses transport arrived of 20, 21st & 13 Squds	
			Attended conference of A.D.V.S. 111 Corp at ETRICOURT.	
			Twelve cases evacuated by 51 M.V.S.	
"	15.7.19		Impulses transport arrived of 224, 225, 231 Field Coy R.E. & 12	
			Sqdn (Pioneer)	

Army Form C. 2118.

WAR DIARY
or
INTELLIGENCE SUMMARY.

(Erase heading not required.)

Instructions regarding War Diaries and Intelligence Summaries are contained in F. S. Regs., Part II. and the Staff Manual respectively. Title pages will be prepared in manuscript.

Place	Date	Hour	Summary of Events and Information	Remarks and references to Appendices
SOREL	16.7.19		Office routine &c. Units 51 MVS & No 2 Section 40 DAC below named to send an V.O. to No 6 V.H. Rouen on reduction of establishment. Capt V R de Bonnis DSO & 40 DuT van detailed to proceed	
"	17.7.19		Opened advanced collecting station & aid station arrived at NURLU (V.26 d.8.6 Sht 57C). Office routine. Infants transport arrived of 14"HL9. Units 181 Bde RFA to impart complete manage cases. 7 in cases evacuated by 51 MVS	
"	18.7.19		Office routine. Infants transport arrived of 12 St Suffolk (121 Bde) D.S.C Bty 296 Bde RFA (attached 40 DAC)	
"	19.7.19		DEtails Infants arrived of D.S.C Bty 296 Bde RFA (attached 40 DAC) all V.O.n at office	
"	20.7.19		Units 51 MVS & complete arrived under treatment & for evacuation	

Army Form C. 2118.

WAR DIARY
or
INTELLIGENCE SUMMARY.
(Erase heading not required.)

Instructions regarding War Diaries and Intelligence Summaries are contained in F. S. Regs., Part II. and the Staff Manual respectively. Title pages will be prepared in manuscript.

Place	Date	Hour	Summary of Events and Information	Remarks and references to Appendices
SOREL	21/4/17		Office routine	
"	22/4/17		7 other ranks evacuated by 51 MVS. Inputs arrival of 18th M.G. Co. who newly arrived from England arranged for medical test (who passed medical test)	
"	23/4/17		Office routine. Inputs arrived in MVS	
"	24/4/17		Inputs arrival of No Dn Train A.S.C.	
"	25/4/17		Inputs arrival of 119th Inf Bde	
"	26/4/17		All O.C.'s at office with return &c	
"	27/4/17		Inputs arrived in 51 MVS	
"	28/4/17		Inputs arrival 17th M.G. Co. under medical test on arrival from England (no medicine)	

Army Form C. 2118.

WAR DIARY
or
INTELLIGENCE SUMMARY.
(Erase heading not required.)

Instructions regarding War Diaries and Intelligence Summaries are contained in F. S. Regs., Part II. and the Staff Manual respectively. Title pages will be prepared in manuscript.

Place	Date	Hour	Summary of Events and Information	Remarks and references to Appendices
SOREL	28/4/17		Inspected aircraft of 231 Field Co. RE. Trench gear inspected by 51 MVS	
"	29/4/17		Office routine. Units 51 MVS to inspect Army vehicles and A.T. medium (with polishing & hyphema etc.)	
"	30/4/17		Units 51 MVS to inspect animals under medical test (movement)	
"	31/4/17		Inspected animals of 178 Bde RFA; condition good.	

W.W. Rowden
Major VS

Army Form C. 2118.

WAR DIARY
or
INTELLIGENCE SUMMARY.
(Erase heading not required.)

DADVS 40th Div   Vol 15

Instructions regarding War Diaries and Intelligence Summaries are contained in F. S. Regs., Part II. and the Staff Manual respectively. Title pages will be prepared in manuscript.

Place	Date	Hour	Summary of Events and Information	Remarks and references to Appendices
SOREL LE GRAND 2nd Sqn W.B.d.S.q	1.8.19		Office routine	
"	2.8.19		All V.O's at office until return ex. Visited 296 Bde R.F.A (att 40 Div) to inspect surplus cases of mange	
"	3.8.19		Inspected animals of 120th Sqn Bde field line transport	
"	4.8.19		Office routine. Stallion cases evacuated to 51 MVS	
"	5.8.19		Inspected animals of B. Echelon 40th D.A.C. (mobile gun)	
"	6.8.19		Inspected animals of 155 Heavy Bty R.G.A (attached 40 Div)	
"	7.8.19		Visited 51 MVS & inspected animals therein	
"	8.8.19		Office routine. Attended inspection by D.D.V.R of surplus horses in the chevaux due to reduction of establishment	

WAR DIARY or INTELLIGENCE SUMMARY

Army Form C. 2118.

Place	Date	Hour	Summary of Events and Information	Remarks and references to Appendices
SOREL LE GRAND	9.8.19		All V.O's at office with monthly returns	
"	10.8.19		Inspected annexes of 229, 224 & 231 Field by R.E & 12 yrds Painters & 139 Field Ambulance	
"	11.8.19		Visited 61 M.V.S. & inspected annexes for evacuation. Report on Phthisis sent in to A.D.V.S III Corps & annexes evacuated to 61 M.V.S.	
"	12.8.19		Inspected annexes of 121 Inf Bde	
"	13.8.19		Inspected annexes of 119 Inf Bde & 135 Field Ambulance	
"	14.8.19		Office routine	
"	15.8.19		D.D. # Orders received to act as president of demand committee for obtaining mules to be used as hand manure (Vide W.O letter 118/R.M/6530 (QM&4) of 29 July 1919)	

(A7092) Wt. W12859/M1293. 75,000. 1/17. D.D. & L., Ltd. Forms/C.2118/14.

Army Form C. 2118.

WAR DIARY
or
INTELLIGENCE SUMMARY.
(Erase heading not required.)

Place	Date	Hour	Summary of Events and Information	Remarks and references to Appendices
SOREL	16.8.19		All V.O.'s at office with returns &c. Ampulis all never of no D.P.C	
"	19.8.19		Ampulis all never of no D.P.C	
"	18.8.19		" " " " 17 F Bde	
			Attended conference at ADVS III Corps H.Q. 13 Cav are units of 51 MVS	
"	19.8.19		Ampulis never of Div H.Q. Signal Co R.E.; 120, 121 Inf Bde; 279 Fd Coy.; 136 F Ambc; 110 U Div Train.	
"	20.8.19		Ampulis never of 122 Bde; 2nd M.L.Cy.; 135, 137 Fd Coy; 231 Fd Ambc RE	
			51 MVS; 119 Inf Bde, 274, 231 Fd Coy RE	
"	21.8.19		Office routine	
"	22.8.19		Committee from III Corps infact horse power permanent vehicles from No Dn artillery	

Army Form C. 2118.

WAR DIARY
or
INTELLIGENCE SUMMARY.

(Erase heading not required.)

Place	Date	Hour	Summary of Events and Information	Remarks and references to Appendices
SOREL	23/8/19		Commute from III Corp reinforcement camp of arrival personnel advises a third never; 1 o details of 96 men arrived in the drawn 62 men french adults and beales	
"	24/8/19		Office routine	
"	25/8/19		Under 51 MVS 5 infants arrived h 51 MVS 18 Case wounded h 51 MVS	
"	26/8/19		Office routine	
"	27/8/19		Attender infants 9 51 MVS h ADVS III Corp	
"	28/8/19		Infants 38 infants made of 40 DHC being returned to Adv. Base	
"	29/8/19		Office routine	
"	30/8/19		DDVS III Corps infants 51 MVS Infants 119 Inf Bn transport	
"	31/8/19		Infants 120 Inf Bn Transport	

MWR

Army Form C. 2118.

WAR DIARY
DADVS INTELLIGENCE SUMMARY. 40th Div.

Vol 16

Place	Date	Hour	Summary of Events and Information	Remarks and references to Appendices
SOREL LE GRAND V.18.d.5.7 (Sh.57C)	1917			
	2.9.17		Impures 1st line transport arrived of 1/21 Inf Bde, all arrived with a few exceptions in fair working condition. 4 broken cases were made to 51 MVS. Impures were made shewing their condition & defects thereupon. Arrived of 115, 120, & 121 Inf Bdes. Visited 63 Sdn Ln at HEUDICOURT to inspect to mutilates arrangements for animal's needs though on inspection of standing, water troughs & supplies animal sich & MVS for intolerable standard.	
	3.9.17		Impures transport arrived of 1/2 Inf Bde (Reserve). Arm of the animal that were all in the open or laving condition that made stables should be commenced without delay. Visited 51 MVS & inspects cases under treatment.	
	4.9.17		Impures arrival of 1/5/ Bde. R.F.A. all arrived in fair working condition.	

Army Form C. 2118.

WAR DIARY
or
INTELLIGENCE SUMMARY.
(Erase heading not required.)

Instructions regarding War Diaries and Intelligence Summaries are contained in F. S. Regs., Part II. and the Staff Manual respectively. Title pages will be prepared in manuscript.

Place	Date	Hour	Summary of Events and Information	Remarks and references to Appendices
SOREL LE GRAND	5.9.17		Inspected Amount of 40 Div Train ASC; all in good condition	
"	6.9.17		All V.O's at Office with returns in	
"	7.9.17		Inspected Amount of 135,137 Field Ambulances, all in good condition. Visited 51 M.V.S. to inspect amount awaiting evacuation	
"	8.9.17		Inspected Amount of 136 Field Ambulance, all in good condition	
"	9.9.17		Inspected medical loadings in course of evacuation for 40 Div Artillery	
"	10.9.17		Inspected Amount of 229, 229, 231 Field Coy R.E., all in fair working condition	
"	11.9.17		Inspected Amount of 244 M.G. Coy & made an good condition but horses neglected. Arranged for additions whereby amount to be kept in ASC till amount were properly cleared up. Inspected loadings of 155 Hy Battn at ETRICOURT being champsfels in order of APVS III Corps previous to evacuation to detraining of unit	

(A7092). Wt W12859/M1293. 75,000. 1/17. D. D. & L., Ltd. Forms/C.2118/14.

Army Form C. 2118.

WAR DIARY
or
INTELLIGENCE SUMMARY.
(Erase heading not required.)

Instructions regarding War Diaries and Intelligence Summaries are contained in F. S. Regs., Part II. and the Staff Manual respectively. Title pages will be prepared in manuscript.

Place	Date	Hour	Summary of Events and Information	Remarks and references to Appendices
SOREL LE GRAND	12.9.17		Accompanied ADMS III Corps on his inspection of 181 Bde RFA & HQ DAC	
"	13.9.17		All V.O.s at office with return	
"	14.9.17		Office routine. Visited 51 MVS to inspect animals under treatment, awaiting evacuation	
"	15.9.17		Orders received from ADMS III Corps to arrange for all animals of No V DAC & No Du Train to be put through the Corps Horse bath at BEAUMETZ. Arrangement made accordingly	
"	16.9.17		Office routine	
"	17.9.17		Visited III Corps Horse Dip at BEAUMETZ to see animals of No V DAC being dipped	

(A7092). Wt W12839/M1293. 75 10.0. 1/17. D. D. & L., Ltd. Forms/C.2118/14.

Army Form C. 2118.

WAR DIARY
~~or~~
INTELLIGENCE SUMMARY.
(Erase heading not required.)

Instructions regarding War Diaries and Intelligence Summaries are contained in F. S. Regs., Part II. and the Staff Manual respectively. Title pages will be prepared in manuscript.

Place	Date	Hour	Summary of Events and Information	Remarks and references to Appendices
SOREL	18.9.17		Mules & animals of 148 Bde R.F.A all in good condition. A number have been evacuated to 51 MVS.	
"	19.9.17		Office routine. Animals arrived in 51 MVS.	
"	20.9.17		All V.O's at office with returns &c. Office routine.	
"	21.9.17		Mules to post line transport animals of 119 Bde, all in good condition. Mules aged & lame animals in 181 Bde R.F.P. recommended for evacuation as not likely to be of further use to retain the unit.	
"	22.9.17		Office routine. A.D.V.S IV Corps visited MVS to inspect mules & glanders case from 63 below Gp. No mules to avoid Cont...	

WAR DIARY or INTELLIGENCE SUMMARY

Army Form C. 2118.

Place	Date	Hour	Summary of Events and Information	Remarks and references to Appendices
SOREL	23.9.19		Office routine	
"	24.9.19		Inspected 1st line transport convoy of 120 Inf Bde, all in fair working condition	
"	25.9.19		Inspected 1st line transport convoy of 121 Inf Bde all in fair working condition. Twelve oxen evacuated to 51 MVS	
"	26.9.19		Office routine	
"	27.9.19		att V.O. at office with return	
"	28.9.19		Office routine	
"	29.9.19		D.D.V.S. inspected 51 MVS and arrival was ordered to Shendi. Convoy discharge 3pm made, diagram of shendi not confirmed	
"	30.9.19		Office routine	

W.W.R.

Army Form C. 2118.

WAR DIARY
or
INTELLIGENCE SUMMARY. 40th Div.

DADVS

Vol 17

Instructions regarding War Diaries and Intelligence Summaries are contained in F. S. Regs., Part II. and the Staff Manual respectively. Title pages will be prepared in manuscript.

(Erase heading not required.)

Place	Date	Hour	Summary of Events and Information	Remarks and references to Appendices
SOREL V.18.d.5.7. Sheet 57 C	1.10.17		Visited 51 MVS & inspected cases for evacuation	
"	2.10.17		Office routine. Office orders. 18 cases evacuated to 51 MVS	
"	3.10.17		Inspected horses of 229, 229, 231 Field Coy RE & 178th Pioneers, all in satisfactory condition	
"	4.10.17		All V.O.'s at office with return &c	
"	5.10.17		Inspected mules of 244 M.G. Coy being transferred to another area of war	
"	6.10.17		Inspected animals of 181 Bde R.F.A. in fair condition. 8 cases evacuated to 51 MVS	
"	7.10.17		Orders received for move of division to another area	
"	8.10.17		Preparation for move	

Army Form C. 2118.

WAR DIARY
or
INTELLIGENCE SUMMARY.
(Erase heading not required.)

Instructions regarding War Diaries and Intelligence Summaries are contained in F. S. Regs., Part II. and the Staff Manual respectively. Title pages will be prepared in manuscript.

Place	Date	Hour	Summary of Events and Information	Remarks and references to Appendices
FOSSEUX	9/10/17		No Div (Lieu R.A) move to Fosseux area ; 51 MUS under VII Corps	
P.10 Sheet 51C	10.10.17		Routine work	
"	11.10.17		Roads moved part of div area & hostile portion of reserve roads & infantry standing	
"	12.10.17		Roads moved rest of div area & hostile portion of roads & infantry standing	
"	13.10.17		51 MUS moved to road & billet at MONCHIET (Q.21. Sheet 51 C)	
"	14.10.17		ADVS VII Corps visited Div H.Q.	
"	15.10.17		Inspected 51 MUS at MONCHIET. Office routine	
"	16.10.17		In company with OC No 11 Div Train inspected 1st line transport arrangement of 119 Inf Bde & 136 F. Ambulance at LOUY & BIEFVILLERS. Condition satisfactory on the whole.	

Army Form C. 2118.

WAR DIARY
or
INTELLIGENCE SUMMARY.
(Erase heading not required.)

Instructions regarding War Diaries and Intelligence Summaries are contained in F. S. Regs., Part II. and the Staff Manual respectively. Title pages will be prepared in manuscript.

Place	Date	Hour	Summary of Events and Information	Remarks and references to Appendices
FOSSEUX	19/10/19		Infantry (with OC and DeTrain) first line transport of 126 Inf Bde & 135 F Amblance at BERNEVILLE & ST EMENCOURT, munition in the whole activities	
"	8/10/19		Infantry (with OC and DeTrain) first line transport of 121 Inf Bde & 134 F Ambulance & 2 44 M.G. Cos at BAREIL, BAVINCOURT, LA HERLIERE. Condition on the whole satisfactory. (No Div again under III Corps for administration)	
"	19.10.19		Proposed & submitted report to OV on 1st line transport of all infantry units	
"	20.10.19		Routine	
"	21.10.19		Routine	
"	22.10.19		Visited 51 MVS at MONCHIET & inspected ammunition & men billets	

Army Form C. 2118.

WAR DIARY
or
INTELLIGENCE SUMMARY.
(Erase heading not required.)

Place	Date	Hour	Summary of Events and Information	Remarks and references to Appendices
FOSSEUX	23/10/19		Inspected command of N°6 Signal C.R.E. including redisposition.	
"	24.10.19		Inspected command of 224, 227 & 231 R.E. & 12 gnl Provin; includes sanitation	
"	25.10.19		V.O. & cl. Office, nil return x	
"	26.10.19		Routine work.	
"	27.10.19		Under 51 M.V.S. 3 inspected animals for evacuation	
"	28.10.19		Routine work	
LUCHEUX T16 Shut 51C	29.10.19		Office moved to Lucheux. 51 M.V.S. at WARLINCOURT LE Pas (Ref 1-1/40.000)	
"	30.10.19		Inspected billets 1 & 51 M.V.S. at WARLINCOURT	
"	31.10.19		Routine work	

W.N. Rowlin
Major A.V.C.
DADVS 4° Dw

WAR DIARY
or
INTELLIGENCE SUMMARY.

(Erase heading not required.)

DADVS 40 Div   Major W.V. ROWSTON. AVC

Army Form C. 2118.

DADVS 40 Army

DADVS 40 Div   Major W.V. ROWSTON. AVC   Va/8

Place	Date	Hour	Summary of Events and Information	Remarks and references to Appendices
LUCHEUX (T.16.2b&3.s.c)	1/4/17		All V.O.s at the with return	
"	2/4/17		Office routine	
"	3/4/17		Visited 51 MVS	
"	4/4/17		Office routine	
"	5/4/17		Animals all but two hundred animals of 119 Inf Bde. condition adequate on the whole; not any little over coming in made standing in their hard cover.	
"	6/4/17		Visited 51 MVS	
"	7/4/17		Animals all but two hundred of 120 Inf Bde; condition animals satisfactory but have overtime but knocked in cover of course. No much standing & deep mud everywhere.	

Army Form C. 2118.

WAR DIARY
or
INTELLIGENCE SUMMARY.
(Erase heading not required.)

Instructions regarding War Diaries and Intelligence Summaries are contained in F.S. Regs., Part II. and the Staff Manual respectively. Title pages will be prepared in manuscript.

Place	Date	Hour	Summary of Events and Information	Remarks and references to Appendices
LUCHEUX	8/4/17		All V.O's at office with returns	
"	9/4/17		Visit 2/n Field Co RE. Establishment of Sus. & LEGER, all around in the open; no horses; equip update with G.	
"	10/4/17		Routine work	
"	11/4/17		Routine work	
"	12/4/17		Trade transfer lorry of 121 Inf Bde	
"	13/4/17		Trade transfer lorry of 14 UC.9. 13 C. Dun	
"	14/4/17		Trade 51 MUS. i no animals evacuated	
"	15/4/17		All V.O's at Ex offici with returns	
"	16/4/17		Duty. G moved to FOSSEUX (P/o Sheet 57c) 51 MUS to MONCHIET Q.11 Sheet 57c	

(A7092). Wt. W12859/M1293. 75,500. 1/17. D.D. & L. Ltd. Forms/C.2118/14.

Army Form C. 2118.

WAR DIARY
or
INTELLIGENCE SUMMARY.
(Erase heading not required)

Instructions regarding War Diaries and Intelligence Summaries are contained in F. S. Regs., Part II. and the Staff Manual respectively. Title pages will be prepared in manuscript.

Place	Date	Hour	Summary of Events and Information	Remarks and references to Appendices
FOSSEUX	14/4/19		Div. H.Q. moved to ACHIET LE PETIT also 51 MUS	
ACHIET-LE-PETIT G.14 (24.5°C)	18/4/19		Orders received to move to HAPLINCOURT; 51 MUS to BEAULENCOURT	
HAPLINCOURT O3 (57C)	19/4/19		Moved to HAPLINCOURT; 51 MUS to No. 4 centre (57C)	
(HAPLINCOURT)			Orders 51 MUS to infants Webs be	
"	21/4/19		Recd H.Q. moved to YPRES (Proc. Huts 57C)	
"	22/4/19		Div. H.Q. moved to BEAUMETZ (J14·57C)	
"			Div. H.Q. moved in afternoon to HAPLINCOURT (1174·57C)	
"			Reg H.Q. " " " NEUVILLE (P11·57C)	
"			And orders to be in readiness to T. Ind Vets · C.C.S. & YPRES	
"			Instruction ont to one units of packing & allowing station sash	
NEUVILLE	23/4/19		Could clean station notified to all V.C.	

(A7092) Wt. W12859/M1293. 75. 9.0. 1/17. D. D. & L., Ltd. Forms/C. 2118/14.

WAR DIARY
or
INTELLIGENCE SUMMARY.

Army Form C. 2118.

Place	Date	Hour	Summary of Events and Information	Remarks and references to Appendices
NEUVILLE	24/11/17		51 MUS move to RUYAUCOURT (P10 Sheet 57c)	
"	25/11/17		Units MUS IV Corps at VILLERS AU FLOS	
"	2/11/17		Units to DAC at TRESCAULT. 15 Cars evacuated to UCCS at YTRES	
"	29/12/17		Div HQ > 51 MUS move to BASSEUX	
BASSEUX (Carrière)	28/12/17		Officer under	
"	29/12/17		Officer under & refused 40 remounts before move to new site	
"	30/12/17		Units developed lines & moved to 1119 Bois	WWR

WAR DIARY or INTELLIGENCE SUMMARY

Army Form C. 2118.

MAJOR WN ROWSTON — A DA DS 40 Div

Vol 19

Place	Date	Hour	Summary of Events and Information	Remarks and references to Appendices
BASSEUX (Lon 1-170 Evo)	1.12.19		ADVS Attended a conference at VI Corps Head Quarters	
"	2.12.19		Orders received for move of DAGMG to BEHAGNIES (H.2. Sheet 57 C) 51 MVS & BOIRY RICTRUDE (S.14 Sheet 51 B)	
BEHAGNIES	3.12.19		Travel to BEHAGNIES and opened offices in nuttish to the staff of 16 Div. Inspected stables, new billets and old arrangements of 51 MVS in their new location at BOIRY RICTRUDE	
"	4.12.19		Inspected mounts of 12 gun (Guns) at BOIECLES, condition good on the whole	
"	6.12.19		Well DAGMG visits BAPAUME to inspect 150 animals arriving for the division from DIEPPE. All in satisfactory condition	
"	7.12.19		Inspected all transport animals of 121 Inf Bde, general condition good on the whole	
"	8.12.19		Attended conference of ADVS VI Corps at Adv HQ at BRETENCOURT	

Army Form C. 2118.

WAR DIARY
or
INTELLIGENCE SUMMARY.
(Erase heading not required.)

Instructions regarding War Diaries and Intelligence Summaries are contained in F. S. Regs., Part II. and the Staff Manual respectively. Title pages will be prepared in manuscript.

Place	Date	Hour	Summary of Events and Information	Remarks and references to Appendices
BEHAGNIES	9.12.19		Offrs routine	
"	10.12.19		Visited 51 MUS to inspect arrangements for evacuation. 15 cases evacuated to 51 MUS	
"	11.12.19		Offrs routine	
"	12.12.19		Inspected bearer arrangements of 13 Essex Regt at HAMELINCOURT. All in good condition.	
"	13.12.19		All S.O.'s at Offrs mess returns. Liden as usual for Div H.Q. to move to BOMIECOURT	
BOMIECOURT (Hq Bu 51)			Moved to BOMIECOURT and opened office	
"	15.12.19		Inspected lines of B.St Bs RFA at HAMELINCOURT, everything in order rather poor.	
"	16.12.19		Visited 51 MUS & inspected all arrangts of Helplessness cases & selected cases to hard cases in lb MUS and carried for dispatch to G in Clare next DUS. Greater numbers increase 199 of 75/11/19	

WAR DIARY
or
INTELLIGENCE SUMMARY.
(Erase heading not required)

Army Form C. 2118.

Place	Date	Hour	Summary of Events and Information	Remarks and references to Appendices
BEHAGNIES COMIECOURT	17.12.17		Visited 14 Car. M. Gun Squadron at ERVILLERS (outside Enfeind & no Br) and inspected mit trench and collected items of regimental information	
"	18.12.19		Inspected all arms of 148 Bde RFA stowed BOIRY ST MARTIN - all in good condition although they have been in the open at the events	
"	19.12.19		In conferm with OC no Dv Train inspected all transpt exempt 1/119 Inf Bde; condtn satisfactory on the whole & so in the open. Detailed report made out & submitted to Div H.Q.	
"	20.12.19		All OC's at office with return &	
"	21.12.19		With OABYMG visited attached detachment stationed at BAPAUME and inspected same	
"	22.12.19		In confirm with OC no Div Train inspected all transpt except 1/121 Inf Bde. Cndtn satisfactory on the whole. Details of report made out & submitted to Div H.Q.	

Army Form C. 2118.

WAR DIARY
INTELLIGENCE SUMMARY.
(Erase heading not required.)

Instructions regarding War Diaries and Intelligence Summaries are contained in F. S. Regs., Part II. and the Staff Manual respectively. Title pages will be prepared in manuscript.

Place	Date	Hour	Summary of Events and Information	Remarks and references to Appendices
ROMIECOURT	23.12.19		In company until OC 40 Div Train inspected all Transport amounted 1 1 2 0 by Bde Transport Officer & cmdkm scrutnized on the whole Details spent remainder at Bde HQ	
"	24.12.19		Inspected all epidemic cases in 51 MUS and relatives there of & cleaners	
"	25.12.19		Xmas day	
"	26.12.19		Routine work	
"	27.12.19		All V.O.s at Ypres each return as	
"	28.12.19		Report received of outbreak of contagion admeath in D.Bn B.H RFA at HAMELINCOURT Visited lines & isolated cases confirmed diagnoses, & drew same in all but all recover ably on to & isolation washing arrangements Inspection of wash lines & mon hop & diagnosis had disable Reports called to A MUS OC	
			8. 40 Div G.i.	
			Inspected stables subject to 100% to cap	
"			Inspected all amount of 1 I V RFA RFA	

WAR DIARY
INTELLIGENCE SUMMARY.

(Erase heading not required.)

Army Form C. 2118.

Place	Date	Hour	Summary of Events and Information	Remarks and references to Appendices
BOMIECOURT	29.12.14		Attended ADVS conference at H.Q. VI Corps	
	30.12.14		Under D.S.1 Bd. RFA to ordered preparation made in Sheepskins or 1 hot drink - water trough	
			Under 2 D.S. 1. Bde RFA to inspect attainable cases (men & horses)	
	31.12.14		Under 51 MVS to inspect Volkhun cases for dentery. to invest is innoculate also all other cases for innoculation	

W.W. Rowston
Major
OOMVS 40 Div

Army Form C. 2118.

WAR DIARY

MAJOR W.N. ROWSTON   DADVS 40 Div

INTELLIGENCE SUMMARY.

(Erase heading not required.)

Vol 20

Place	Date	Hour	Summary of Events and Information	Remarks and references to Appendices
GOMIECOURT Army Huts 50	1.1.18		Inspected animals of 40" D.A.C. at HAMELINCOURT	
"	2.1.18		Inspected animals, cases in D.V.Hs, R.F.A. at " "	
"			Office routine	
"	3.1.18		All V.O.s at office, whom detailed re	
"	4.1.18		Inspected animals of 229 Field Coy RE at ST LEGER	
"	5.1.18		DDVS' Attended conference at VI Corps H.Q.	
"	6.1.18		Visited 51 MVS & inspected animals for evacuation also epidemic cases under treatment	
BEHAGNIES Hq Huts 50	7.1.18		Div H.Q. moved to BEHAGNIES	
			26 cases evacuated by 51 MVS	

WAR DIARY
INTELLIGENCE SUMMARY.

Army Form C. 2118.

Place	Date	Hour	Summary of Events and Information	Remarks and references to Appendices
BEHAGNIES	8.1.18		Ambulance transport consists of 1 x 20 cwt Bd & one extra under construction at Bryant Camp (near MORY).	
"	9.1.18		In conference with OC 40 Dn Train respecting transport arrangements of 135, 136, & 139 Field Ambulances; approved report on same to Dn HQ.	
"	10.1.18		All OC's at office and returns &c. Under D.151 Bde R.F.A. 2 ambulance demountable cars, eleven pulled out as unsvcd.	
"	11.1.18		In conference with OC 40 Dn Train respecting transport arrangements of 12 Yorks (Pioneers) at MORY & 244 M.G. Coy at ERVILLERS. Report on same sent to Dn HQ.	
"	12.1.18		Attended A.D.M.S. conference at H.Q. VI Corps.	
"	13.1.18		Under 51 MOS at evacuation cases for evacuation; also ophthalmic case under treatment.	

Army Form C. 2118.

WAR DIARY
or
INTELLIGENCE SUMMARY.

(Erase heading not required.)

Instructions regarding War Diaries and Intelligence Summaries are contained in F.S. Regs., Part II. and the Staff Manual respectively. Title pages will be prepared in manuscript.

Place	Date	Hour	Summary of Events and Information	Remarks and references to Appendices
BEHAGNIES	14.1.18		Ampules transport consists of 724 5231 Field Coy RE & ERVILLERS & MSR)	
			25 Cars evacuated to 51 MVS	
	16.1.18		Ampules removed to No 4 Dn on arrival at BAPAUME.	
	16.1.18		Officer routine	
	17.1.18		All W.O.'s & NCOs met return to Units. No 4 Du Tram & Equipment & Ampules near stable under construction.	
	18.1.18		Officer routine	
	19.1.18		Attended conference at VI Corps HQ. Visits 181 Bde RFA at Hamelincourt	
	20.1.18		Ampules 9th & 4th RFA (HFA Bdg) also Ukran uml Visits 145 Bde RFA at Bn St Marie. Ampules consists for evacuation in 51 MVS	
	21.1.18		Proceeded on leave for 14 days.	

WW Pemerton
Maj RAMC

(A7692) Wt. W12859/M1293. 75,000. 1/17. D. D. & L., Ltd. Forms/C.2118/14.

Army Form C. 2118.

WAR DIARY
INTELLIGENCE SUMMARY.

MAJOR W.N. ROWSTON A/DADVS or DADVS 40th Div. Feb 1918

(Erase heading not required.)

Place	Date	Hour	Summary of Events and Information	Remarks and references to Appendices
BEHAGNIES (H2.5b57c)	6/2/18		Arrived at Dn H.Q on return from leave	
	7/2/18		All V.O's at Office with returns etc. Inspected transport animals of 11 K.O.R.L on departure from 40 Div. Inspected animals of 181 Bde R.F.A cases of mange known & now in the stable which I saw over on leave.	
	8/2/18		Visited S.M.V.S at BOIRY ST MARTIN, inspected animals under treatment & awaiting evacuation	
	9/2/18		Attended ADVS VI Corps conference at BRETENCOURT.	
	10/2/18		Office routine	
	11/2/18		Visited S.M.V.S. Inspected 34 animals awaiting evacuation that day	
	12/2/18		Inspected animals of Mn. Section 40th DAC all in good condition	

Army Form C. 2118.

WAR DIARY
INTELLIGENCE SUMMARY.
(Erase heading not required.)

Place	Date	Hour	Summary of Events and Information	Remarks and references to Appendices
GOMIECOURT (Arg 51-54 c)	13.2.18		Div. H.Q. move to Gomiecourt all V.O.'s at office until return &c.	
"	14.2.18		Inspected command of 1/1 Royal Pioneers 229 323 Field Coy R.E. all in satisfactory condition.	
"	15.2.18		Attended conference at A.D.V.S. VI Corps. Made B Bh wagon lines 151 Bde R.F.A. to inspect anfules mange &c. Inspected animals 229 Field Coy R.E. at HAMELINCOURT all in satisfactory condition.	
"	17.2.18		Visited 51 M.V.S. & inspected animals for evacuation, also men billets and horse &c. (changing)	
"	18.2.18		Attended B.O.C. & inspection of fresh lines transport of 1/120 Inf Bde. at BLAIREVILLE.	

Army Form C. 2118.

WAR DIARY
or
INTELLIGENCE SUMMARY.
(Erase heading not required.)

Instructions regarding War Diaries and Intelligence Summaries are contained in F. S. Regs., Part II. and the Staff Manual respectively. Title pages will be prepared in manuscript.

Place	Date	Hour	Summary of Events and Information	Remarks and references to Appendices
BONNIEUX	19/4/18		Inspected armament of No 1 section 110th DAC; all in excellent condition	
"	20/4/18		Attended divisional general inspection of first line transport of 117 my Bde at MERCATEL	
			All V.G. at Offrs mess return cr	
"	21/4/18		Attended divisional general inspection of first line transport of 171 my Bde at HAMELINCOURT.	
			Inspected enfilade range cases in A+B Bty, 111 Bde RFA.	
	22/4/18		Office routine	
	23/4/18		Attended A.D.V.S. VI Corps conference at BRETENCOURT	
	24/4/18		Visited S.M.V.S. and inspected team under treatment + awaiting evacuation	
	25/4/18		Office routine cr	
			3 animal evacuated by S.M.V.S.	

WAR DIARY
or
INTELLIGENCE SUMMARY

Army Form C. 2118.

Place	Date	Hour	Summary of Events and Information	Remarks and references to Appendices
BOMIECOURT	26/4/18		Impletes arrival of B. Echelon to V DAC at HAMELINCOURT. All in good condition.	
"	27/4/18		Orders received for 40 V Dn to move to BASSEUX area. 5 M.O.S to go to BELLACOURT. (MAP REF. LENS 1/20,000)	
"	28/4/18		Moved to BASSEUX a opened office.	
	28/4/18			

WN Rawlins
Major RA

Army Form C. 2118.

MAJOR W.N. ROWSTON WAR DIARY MARCH 1918
D.A.D.M.S. 40th Div. INTELLIGENCE SUMMARY.

Place	Date	Hour	Summary of Events and Information	Remarks and references to Appendices
BASSEUX (Ref Reform II)	1/3/18		Office routine	
"	2/3/18		Attended a conference at Hqrs 1 A.D.V.S. II Corps at BRETENCOURT	
"	3/3/18		Moved 5 /M.V.S. from BEUGNÂTRE to new outfit at MONCHIET	
"	4/3/18		Inspected Command of 40 M.G. Batt. at HENDECOURT; all in good condition	
"	5/3/18		Inspected command of No 4 Sqdn 6 R.E.; condition satisfactory	
"	6/3/18		Inspected transport command 1/3 E. Surr. 1/5 Wall. 1/21 M'sex (119 Bde) W- BLAIRVILLE - HENDECOURT; condition satisfactory 39 Cases evacuated to 5 /M.V.S.	
"	7/3/18		All U.O's & Offrs noted returns &c	

Army Form C. 2118.

WAR DIARY
or
INTELLIGENCE SUMMARY.
(Erase heading not required.)

Instructions regarding War Diaries and Intelligence Summaries are contained in F. S. Regs., Part II. and the Staff Manual respectively. Title pages will be prepared in manuscript.

Place	Date	Hour	Summary of Events and Information	Remarks and references to Appendices
BASSEUX	8/3/15		Visited M.O. Du Train at ST. AMAND to inspect him for sanitary for drugs & debility	
"	9/3/15		Attended conference at H.Q. VI Corps	
"	10/9/15		Got invited 136 F. Ambulance at BLAIREVILLE to investigate complaint by "home made" VI Corps as to stretcher management and condition of the wounds; found on exam. the complaint & wounds in good condition. Visited transfer lines of wounds of 121 Inf. Bde.; wounds in good condition	
"	11/3/15		Inspected wounds of 148 Bde. R.F.A. at SOUASTRE; condition very fair	
"	10/3/15		Officer wounded	
"	13/3/15		Visited 31 M.V.S. the Hands and no complaints until some forward of the division into the reserve	

(A7092). Wt. W12839/M1293. 75,000. 1/17. D. D. & L., Ltd. Forms/C.2118/14.

Army Form C. 2118.

WAR DIARY
or
INTELLIGENCE SUMMARY.
(Erase heading not required.)

Instructions regarding War Diaries and Intelligence Summaries are contained in F. S. Regs., Part II. and the Staff Manual respectively. Title pages will be prepared in manuscript.

Place	Date	Hour	Summary of Events and Information	Remarks and references to Appendices
BASSEUX	14/3/18		All V.O.s & Offrs met return to 12 and minutes & 51 MUS	
"	15/3/18		Vardis major hour 1 181 Bde RFA at MOYENNE AVESNE ? condition of animals seen	
"	16/3/18		Attended ADV.S. II Corps conference	
"	17/3/18		Vardis 51 MUS & Handicourt	
"	18/3/18		Offr surveils se	
"	19/3/18		Offr surveils se	
"	20/3/18		Int removed from at BOISIEUX-AU-MONT & impels remounts for its division	

Army Form C. 2118.

WAR DIARY
or
INTELLIGENCE SUMMARY.

(Erase heading not required.)

Instructions regarding War Diaries and Intelligence Summaries are contained in F. S. Regs., Part II. and the Staff Manual respectively. Title pages will be prepared in manuscript.

Place	Date	Hour	Summary of Events and Information	Remarks and references to Appendices
BIHUCOURT	21/9/18		V.C. at offrs mess & return or	
"	22/9/18		Moved to BUCQUOY : 51 MUS moved to ADINFER	
BUCQUOY	23/9/18		Visited 51 MUS at ADINFER	
"			Moved Offrs to SOUASTRE : 51 MUS to ST AMAND	
SOUASTRE	24/9/18		{ Seven to military schedules & conduct move of units with unit }	
"	25			
"	26			
"	27		Moved Offrs to LUCHEUX : 51 MUS to HUMBERCAMP	
"	28		Moved to CHELERS : 51 MUS to HERLIN-LE-VERT	
LUCHEUX	29/9/18			

WAR DIARY
or
INTELLIGENCE SUMMARY.

Army Form C. 2118.

Place	Date	Hour	Summary of Events and Information	Remarks and references to Appendices
CHELERS	3/5/18		Men under	
	3/5/18		Move to MERVILLE (Blvd Herbert S.A.) 51 M.B. mov to LILLERS (wards to MERVILLE)	

W W Rankin
Maj xx

Army Form C. 2118.

WAR DIARY
INTELLIGENCE SUMMARY.

MAJOR W.N ROWSTON — DADVS 40th Div

APRIL 1918

(Erase heading not required.)

Place	Date	Hour	Summary of Events and Information	Remarks and references to Appendices
MERVILLE (Sheet Hazebrouck 5A)	1/4/18		51 MVS moved to TRou BAYARD & other new premises vacated by MVS of 50th Div (Give Sheet No 36)	
"	2/4/18		Div H.Q. moved to CROIX-DU-BAC (Sheet 36 G.6.c)	
CROIX-DU-BAC (Sheet 36 G.6.c)	3/4/18		DDVS. 1st Army visited 40 Div. Inspected arm of the division drawn from 51st MVS	
"	4/4/18		All V.O.'s & offrs with return. Inspected animals of 137 Fd Ambulance & 231 Field Co R.E.	
"	5/4/18		Visited 51 MVS & inspected cases for inoculation (9 animals)	
"	6/4/18		Inspected transport animal of No 29 RB also 13 Yorks & 12 Suffolk. 23 Cases inoculated by 51 MVS.	
"	7/4/18		Office routine	

Army Form C. 2118.

WAR DIARY
or
INTELLIGENCE SUMMARY.
(Erase heading not required.)

Instructions regarding War Diaries and Intelligence Summaries are contained in F. S. Regs., Part II. and the Staff Manual respectively. Title pages will be prepared in manuscript.

Place	Date	Hour	Summary of Events and Information	Remarks and references to Appendices
CROIX DU BAC	8/4/18		Infantry consists of 40th Signal Coy R.E.	
"	9/4/18		Infantry Wirefront consists of 20 Motors and 40 Pu. H.Q. coupled to leave km du Bac by trucks prior to proceed to DOULIEU & VIEUX BERGUIN, news heard speaker at LA MOTTE AU BOIS (36 A.D.30.6.95) 2 51 M.U.S. to LA RUE du BOIS (36 A.E.97.b)	
LA MOTTE AU BOIS	10/4/18		Vrales 51 MUS impulse ornach for evacuation (22)	
"	11/4/18		Dn H.Q. move to AU-SOUVERAIN (Sheet 3 A.d.11.b). 2-1 M.U.S. to HONDEGHEM (Hazebrouck 5 A)	
AU SOUVERAIN	12/4/18		No much trouble over to the military situation	
"	13/4/18		Dn H.Q. move to RENESCURE (Hazebrouck 5 A)	
RENESCURE	14/4/18		Dn H.Q. 251 MUS to LONGUENESSE (B Hazebrouck 5 A)	

Army Form C. 2118.

WAR DIARY
or
INTELLIGENCE SUMMARY.
(Erase heading not required.)

Instructions regarding War Diaries and Intelligence Summaries are contained in F. S. Regs., Part II. and the Staff Manual respectively. Title pages will be prepared in manuscript.

Place	Date	Hour	Summary of Events and Information	Remarks and references to Appendices
LONGUENESSE	15/4/18		Units 51 M.V.S.	
"	16/4/18		Dr H G moved to WIZERNES (New 36 D.E.8.b.9.9.)	
WIZERNES	17/4/18		Reported to A.D.O.S. VIII Corps at CASSEL	
"	18/4/18		V.O. & office visits return &c	
"	19/4/18		Units No 23 Vet Hospital at ST. OMER	
"	20/4/18		Ampules transport arrived of 170 Inf Bde	
"	21/4/18		Ampules transport arrived of 171 Inf Bde	
			Capt S Hunter AVC (SR) reported his arrival in relief of Capt G.C. Larvell or (S.R) when on been transferred to No 10 Vet Hospital	
"	22/4/18		Units 51 M.V.S.	
			Capt Larvell reported his departure to No 10. V.H.	
			Units 51 MVS a item near kitchen at BOISDINGHEM	

WAR DIARY
or
INTELLIGENCE SUMMARY

Place	Date	Hour	Summary of Events and Information	Remarks and references to Appendices
WIZERNES	23/4/18		Routine work	
	24/4/18		Instructions received that no Dn is to be returned to "Personnel establishment" for a training draw. AVC personnel to remain with the drawn the further adm ? 51 MVS to remain intact, to be employed under adm of 1 Army	
	25/4/18		Routine work	
	26/4/18		Visits No 5 V.H and Remount Depot at Calais. Two complaints Bdn. Received from no Dn. > plans at chaput of VWS Coys. The adm for return to trenches establishment from Employment completed	
	27/4/18		Routine work	
	28/4/18		" "	
	29/4/18		Div H.Q move to SI OMER	
	30/4/18			51 MUSB SENINGHEM (Hazebrouck's A 24, 45, 45) WN Rowlin Major AVC

Army Form C. 2118.

WAR DIARY MAY. 1918
of Major W.N ROWSTON
INTELLIGENCE SUMMARY. DADVS. 40th Dn

Instructions regarding War Diaries and Intelligence
Summaries are contained in F. S. Regs., Part II.
and the Staff Manual respectively. Title pages
will be prepared in manuscript.

(Erase heading not required.)

Vol 2 Bdy

Place	Date	Hour	Summary of Events and Information	Remarks and references to Appendices
St OMER	1.5.18		Office routine.	
"	2.5.18		V.O. at office with return	
"	3.5.18		Office routine. 6 S.I. MVS	
			3 Cars evacuate 6 40 M.G. Batt which is being taken up 3 pulks out	
"	4.5.18		Impules camel of 40 M.G. Batt which is being taken up 3 pulks out	
			Cannot wait to move & sent own to MVS	
			S.I. MVS move to St MOMELIN Sheet 27A R.11.c.	
"	5.5.18		Visited S.I. MVS at St Momelin and impules killed &c	
	—		9 Cases evacuated to S.I MVS	
"	6.5.18		Routine work	
			8 Cases evacuated to S.I M.V.S	
"	7.5.18		Impules horse of 40 U Signal Co R.E.	
"	8.5.18		Withdrew with mullet of 40 M.G. Batt which has been taken up	

(A7092) Wt W12859/M1293 75,10,00. 1/17. D. D. & L., Ltd. Forms/C.2118/14.

Army Form C. 2118.

WAR DIARY
or
INTELLIGENCE SUMMARY.

(Erase heading not required.)

Instructions regarding War Diaries and Intelligence Summaries are contained in F. S. Regs., Part II. and the Staff Manual respectively. Title pages will be prepared in manuscript.

Place	Date	Hour	Summary of Events and Information	Remarks and references to Appendices
St OMER	9/5/18		DDS at office with returns &c	
"	10/5/18		Visited 51 MUS at ST MOMELIN and horsepool of 119 and Bde & in yard. Prisoners at MEURIET & BONNETHEM. Sick horses evacuated by 51 M.V.S. Routine work	
"	11/5/18		51 M.V.S. move to LE TOM Abt 29 I.31.c.3.3. Site to near unit engaged in preparing the # WINNEZEELE line and as being administered by 40th Divn. Received instructions to act temporarily as ADVS VII Corps during absence of ADVS with remainder of army. Seen another vet with relieve Pm̄ Adv Base Depot Vety Stores.	
"	12/5/18		Visited VII Corps HQ & disposed of matters requiring attention in ADVS office	
"	13/5/18		Routine work	

Army Form C. 2118.

WAR DIARY
or
INTELLIGENCE SUMMARY.
(Erase heading not required.)

Place	Date	Hour	Summary of Events and Information	Remarks and references to Appendices
ST OMER	14/5/18		Visited H.Q. VII Corps & dispersed of officer work in ADMS office.	
			First saw Lieutenant of 118, 119, 121 3rd Bdes 31st Regd. Proceed also No. 3, 4 Coy. No. 1 DuTram left the division for ETAPLES.	
			Capt. J.R. Ragh. AMC (TC) left in with charge of them.	
			Two cars evacuated by 51 MUS	
	15/5/18		Routine work	
	16/5/18		At VII Corps H.Q.	
	17/5/18		Visited 51 MUS at LE TOM	
	18/5/18		At VII Corps H.Q.	
			S.A.A. Section No. D.A.C. left the division on being disbanded	
	19/5/18		Routine work	

Army Form C. 2118.

WAR DIARY
or
INTELLIGENCE SUMMARY

(Erase heading not required.)

Instructions regarding War Diaries and Intelligence Summaries are contained in F. S. Regs., Part II. and the Staff Manual respectively. Title pages will be prepared in manuscript.

Place	Date	Hour	Summary of Events and Information	Remarks and references to Appendices
ST OMER	20/5/18		At VII Corps H.Q. 16 Can evacuated to 51 MUS	
"	21/5/18		Under 51 MUS at LE TOM.	
"	22/5/18		At VII Corps H.Q.	
"	23/5/18		Office routine. Routine work	
"	24/5/18		At VII Corps H.Q.	
"	25/5/18		Office routine	
"	26/5/18		Under 51 MUS	
"	27/5/18		14 Can evacuated to 51 MUS	

Army Form C. 2118.

WAR DIARY
or
INTELLIGENCE SUMMARY.

(Erase heading not required.)

Instructions regarding War Diaries and Intelligence Summaries are contained in F. S. Regs., Part II. and the Staff Manual respectively. Title pages will be prepared in manuscript.

Place	Date	Hour	Summary of Events and Information	Remarks and references to Appendices
ST OMER	28/5/15		At VII Corps HQ	
			135 & 136 Field Ambulances left 40th Div to join 4 "Lowland" Infantry Div	
"	29/5/15		Visited 134 F Ambulance at KINDERBEECK	
"	30/5/15		Return made out	
"	31/5/15		Render work; the delay of animal transport of the dio a more down to make 500 animals emergents than a little wonder to be done for the present	

W N Rowden
Major A.D.

WAR DIARY
INTELLIGENCE SUMMARY

of D.A.D.V.S 40th Dn
MAJOR W.N. ROWSTON
June 1918

Place	Date	Hour	Summary of Events and Information	Remarks and references to Appendices
ST-OMER	1/6/18		Gunning to 40 Div Horse Show returned to the train of a trenching drawn and no Div Artillery being detailed there as very few horses left with the chasseur & very little note observation work to be done.	
"	2/6/18		D/y DVS VII Corps inspected 51 MVS	
"	3/6/18		Office routine	
LEDERZEELE Sh 27 E.7.a	4/6/18		Dn H.Q. moved to LEDERZEELE (Sheet 27 E.7.a.) Office routine	
"	5/6/18		Inspected 234 Field Co R.E. at U.1.b.6.9. (Sh. 27)	
"	6/6/18		With A.D.V.S VII Corps inspected Mob Vy A.S.C. 154 F Ambulance 224, 231 Field Coy R.E.	
"	7/6/18		Office routine	
"	8/6/18		Attended conference at Office of A.D.V.S VII Corps	

Army Form C. 2118.

WAR DIARY
or
INTELLIGENCE SUMMARY.

(Erase heading not required.)

Instructions regarding War Diaries and Intelligence Summaries are contained in F. S. Regs., Part II. and the Staff Manual respectively. Title pages will be prepared in manuscript.

Place	Date	Hour	Summary of Events and Information	Remarks and references to Appendices
LEDERZEELE	9/6/15		Visited 51 M.D.S	
"	9/6/15		Routine work	
"	10/6/15		" "	
"	11/6/15		No "D" in town moved up again to full strength unit German Battalion & infantry transport in full need for an infantry Kitchen	
"	12/6/15		Routine work	
"	13/6/15		Routine work, weekly return rendered	
"	14/6/15		Routine work	
"	15/6/15		"	
"	16/6/15		Moved 51 M.D.S. to St Momelin (Sheet 27A. R.11.c)	
"	17/6/15		Infantry transport amount of 1.10 German Br KOSB 1509 B. 15 - KOYLI Cameron Highlanders 1209 R Bde	
			Funnels refused on account to H.Q. & ADV.S VIII Corps	

Army Form C. 2118.

WAR DIARY
or
INTELLIGENCE SUMMARY.
(Erase heading not required.)

Instructions regarding War Diaries and Intelligence Summaries are contained in F. S. Regs., Part II. and the Staff Manual respectively. Title pages will be prepared in manuscript.

Place	Date	Hour	Summary of Events and Information	Remarks and references to Appendices
LEDERZEELE	18/6/18		Visited 51 MUS	
"	19/6/18		Inspected 2/9 Field a RE	
"	20/6/18		Office routine, return &c	
"	21/6/18		"	
"	22/6/18		"	
"	23/6/18		H.Q. 40 Div moved to RENESCURE (Shed 29 T & O d) + 51 MUS LYNDE (Shed 36 a. B.11.a)	
RENESCURE LYNDE	24/6/18		Visited the 1 ADVS XV Corps & STAPLE infantes on Suspected killed &c	
"	25/6/18		Capt. Bayley RTC shown from CVCQ Common Inspected transport animal 1/23 Lan. Rn Lane Fusiliers	
"	26/6/18		1/4 " Wigton Regt & 12/1 Inf Bde 1/5 " 23 Cheshire Regt Returned report to H.Q. 40 Div + ADVS XV Corps	

Army Form C. 2118.

WAR DIARY
or
INTELLIGENCE SUMMARY
(Erase heading not required.)

Place	Date	Hour	Summary of Events and Information	Remarks and references to Appendices
RENESCURE	27/6/18		Routine work, returns &c	
"	28/6/18		Inspected transfer convoy 13 Gen Hos (march fm) 13 " " Eleven Rgs } 119 Inf Bn 12 " " N Staff Regt 12 " " " N Staff Regt	
			Submitted report to A.D.V.S VIII Corps & H.Q. 40 Div	
"	29/6/18		Visited 51 M.V.S	
"	30/6/18		Routine work.	

W.D. Rowlin
Major AVC

Army Form C. 2118.

WAR DIARY
INTELLIGENCE SUMMARY.

MAJOR W.N. ROWSTON or DADYS 40 Dn

July 1918

SA 26

Place	Date	Hour	Summary of Events and Information	Remarks and references to Appendices
RENESCURE SW 29 T.20.d	1/7/18		Inspected No 3 Coy 40 Dn Train & submits report to Dn H.Q	
"	2/7/18		Inspected No 4 Coy 40 Dn Train	
"	3/7/18		Routine work	
"	4/7/18		V.O's at Офис with return &c	
"			Inspected annual of No 2 Coy 40 Dn Train and submits report to Dn H.Q.	
"			S.A.A. Section 40 DAC gave the demo on its being reformed	
"	5/7/18		Inspected annual of 135 Fd. Ambulance	
"	6/7/18		Inspected annual of 135 & 137 Fd. Ambulances & Ambulance of pack to D.H.Q.	
"	7/7/18		Routine work	
"	8/7/18		Inspected equipt annual of 12th Field Co R.E. and submits report to D.H.Q.	

WAR DIARY
or
INTELLIGENCE SUMMARY.

Army Form C. 2118.

Place	Date	Hour	Summary of Events and Information	Remarks and references to Appendices
RENESCURE	9/11/18		Inspected horses of 231 Fd & R.E. & submitted report to D.H.Q.	
"	10/11/18		Inspected horses of very Field & R.E. & S.A.A. Sectn. No 4 D.A.C. & submitted report to D.H.Q.	
"	11/11/18		Routine work. V.O. at office until advance	
"	12/11/18		Visited Divisional horses of 23rd Divn. & 113 Immobile Section to inspect animals for evacuation which had been commenced in 1st & 2nd S.O.C. at the request of the previous day	
"	13/11/18		Visited divisional horses of S.A.A. Section No 4 D.A.C.	
"	14/11/18		Routine work	
"	15/11/18		Attended head qts. No. 3 G.H.S.C. for the examination of cold shoers as to their fitness for shoeing smith	

WAR DIARY
or
INTELLIGENCE SUMMARY.

Army Form C. 2118.

(Erase heading not required.)

Place	Date	Hour	Summary of Events and Information	Remarks and references to Appendices
RENESCURE	14/7/18		Orders respecting to Div Commands of 51 M.V.S.	
"	17/7/18		Routine work	
"	18/7/18		Infale amount of No 85 Signal Co RE submitted approved by D.H.Q.	
"	19/7/18		V.D. at Office work returns	
"	20/7/18		Office returns	
"	21/7/18		Under 51 M.V.S. to inspect animals for evacuation	
"	22/7/18		Routine work	
"	23/7/18		Under 51 M.V.S., 120 Fd H.Q. & handed over 7 119 Inf. Bde.	

WAR DIARY
or
INTELLIGENCE SUMMARY.

Army Form C. 2118.

Place	Date	Hour	Summary of Events and Information	Remarks and references to Appendices
RENESCURE	24/9/18		3 Officers transport command of 120 & 2nd Bde submitted report to DHQ	
"	25/9/18		Officer in return x	
"	26/9/18		Officers transport command of 121 2nd Bde submitted report to DHQ	
"	27/9/18		Routine work	
"	28/9/18		Routine work	
"	29/9/18		Visited 31 MVS to inspect animals for evacuation	
"	30/9/18		Routine work	
"	29/9/18		Routine work	

W W Renton
Major

Army Form C. 2118.

WAR DIARY
or
INTELLIGENCE SUMMARY

MAJOR W.N. ROWSTON DADVS 40 Dn

August 1918

Place	Date	Hour	Summary of Events and Information	Remarks and references to Appendices
RENESCURE Sh.9.d T 20.d	1/8/18		Inspected Horses of 2, 3 & 4 Coy 40 Dn Train & admitted report to DDVS	
"	2/8/18		Office routine	
"	3/8/18		Inspected horses & mules of 119 Inf Bde & admitted report to DHQ	
"	4/8/18		Visited 51 MVS & inspected animals for evacuation	
"	5/8/18		Office routine	
"	6/8/18		Inspected animals of 120 Inf Bde & admitted report to DHQ	
"	7/8/18		Routine visits	
"	8/8/18		V.O. at office until return &c	

Army Form C. 2118.

WAR DIARY
or
INTELLIGENCE SUMMARY.
(Erase heading not required.)

Instructions regarding War Diaries and Intelligence Summaries are contained in F. S. Regs., Part II. and the Staff Manual respectively. Title pages will be prepared in manuscript.

Place	Date	Hour	Summary of Events and Information	Remarks and references to Appendices
RENESCURE	9/8/18		Impacts transport amounts of 135, 136 & 137 Fd Ambulance & submitted report to D.H.Q.	
"	10/8/18		Attended conference of A.D.V.S. XV Corps at STAPLE. Inocd 51 M.V.S. & inspected same for innoculation	
"	11/8/18		Office routine	
"	12/8/18		Inspected transport amounts of 227 Field Coy R.E. & submitted report to D.H.Q.	
"	13/8/18		Office routine	
"	14/8/18		Inspected transport amount of 224, 231 Field Coy R.E. & submitted report to D.H.Q.	
"	15/8/18		V.O.'s office not returned in	
"	16/8/18		Inspected amounts of S.A.A. Park & M.D.A.C. & submitted report to D.H.Q.	

WAR DIARY
or
INTELLIGENCE SUMMARY.

Army Form C. 2118.

Place	Date	Hour	Summary of Events and Information	Remarks and references to Appendices
RENESCURE	17/11/18		Office routine	
"	18/11/18		Visited 51 MVS & inspected cars for evacuation	
"	19/11/18		Orders in regard to No Dn Hors Show	
"	20/11/18		Office routine	
"	21/11/18		Attended information to C in C Committee of handed from room	
"	22/11/18		BAVINCHOVE V.O.'s of offices until return x	
"	23/11/18		Routine work	
WALLON-CAPPEL	24/11/18		Moved HQ to WALLON-CAPPEL 2S, MVS & STIE PER 36A/Cz 033 Attended Mtg O.C.s Conference D.H.Q.	
27/V.29				
"	25/11/18		Visited 51 MVS & inspected horses in their new lines	

WAR DIARY
or
INTELLIGENCE SUMMARY.

(Erase heading not required.)

Army Form C. 2118.

Place	Date	Hour	Summary of Events and Information	Remarks and references to Appendices
WALLON-CAPPEL	26/8/15		Proceeded to gmty. at 31st Div. Hors Shows	
"	27/8/15		Office work	
	28/8/15		Routine work	
	29/8/15		Arrangs new location of MDS at myf 030 B.22	
	30/8/15		51 MDS moves to new location which is near to mists	
	31/8/15		Welcome home dinner at mess in vicinity of Steenvoorde of 120 W. Reds.	
			Infants arrival of 110 M.M.G.s	
			Attends G.O.C's conference at D.H.Q.	

W.H. Rusten
Major RAMC

Army Form C. 2118.

WAR DIARY
INTELLIGENCE SUMMARY

MAJOR W.N. ROWSTON — DADVS 40 Dn

Sept 1918

Place	Date	Hour	Summary of Events and Information	Remarks and references to Appendices
WALLON CAPPEL	1/9/18		Attended inspection of 1st Line transport of 119 Inf. Bde. by Divnl Commander	
"	2/9/18		Inspected animals of 119 Inf. Waclin. Visited 51 MVS. Inspected car for evacuation	
LAMOTTE AU BOIS 564/D30	3/9/18		D.H.Q. moved to LA MOTTE AU BOIS. Visited Horse Effect store.	
"	4/9/18		Visited horse lines of 121 Inf. Bde at DOULIEU. 51 MVS moved to 364/E 11.a.2.4	
"	5/9/18		Inspected animals of No Depot & RE. Indent for remounts expected to DHQ. Visited 51 MVS. Inspected Mule oc	
"	6/9/18		Office routine	

Army Form C. 2118.

WAR DIARY
or
INTELLIGENCE SUMMARY.
(Erase heading not required.)

Instructions regarding War Diaries and Intelligence Summaries are contained in F. S. Regs., Part II. and the Staff Manual respectively. Title pages will be prepared in manuscript.

Place	Date	Hour	Summary of Events and Information	Remarks and references to Appendices
LA MOTTE AU BOIS	1/9/15		Officer routine (very wet day)	
"	8/9/15		Under transport lines of 1 mo 2nd Bde + 2NA CON CAPPEL	
"	9/9/15		Officer routine (very wet day)	
"	10/9/15		Under 51 M.V.S. inspected animals for evacuation (very wet week)	
"	11/9/15		Officer routine (endurance met muscular)	
"	12/9/15		CW U.O.s at Office watch actions &c	
"	13/9/15		Under transport lines 113th Clothes + S.R Horse (119 Bde)	
"	14/9/15		Inspected transport animals of 119 Inf Bde submitted report to D.H.Q.	
"	15/9/15- 19/9/15		Officer routine to exchange with O.C. 51 M.V.S. to 1st at from Rethel on leave	

WVR

Army Form C. 2118.

WAR DIARY
or
INTELLIGENCE SUMMARY.

(Erase heading not required.)

Instructions regarding War Diaries and Intelligence Summaries are contained in F. S. Regs., Part II. and the Staff Manual respectively. Title pages will be prepared in manuscript.

Place	Date	Hour	Summary of Events and Information	Remarks and references to Appendices
LA MOTTE AU BOIS.	16/9/18		Took over duties of D.A.D.V.S. for Major N N Rowston whilst on leave.	
"	17/9/18		Attended Office.	
"	18/9/18		Inspected 121 Infantry Officers Transport Lines, submitted report to D.H.Q. and A.D.V.S., XV Corps.	
"	19/9/18		Inspected 7 cases evacuated by 51 M.V.S. V.Os at Office with returns.	
"	19/9/18		Inspected Field Companies R.E. and Divisional Train, submitted reports to D.H.Q. and A.D.V.S., XV Corps.	
"	20/9/18		Sent returns away. Inspected two Field Ambulances, submitted reports to D HQ and A.D.V.S., XV Corps.	
"	21/9/18		Inspected 6 cases evacuated by 51 M.V.S.	
"	22/9/18		Inspected 7 cases evacuated by 51 M.V.S.	
"	23/9/18		Inspected remounts for the Division at WALLON CAPPEL. Inspected 5 cases evacuated by 51 M.V.S.	

Army Form C. 2118.

WAR DIARY
or
INTELLIGENCE SUMMARY.

(Erase heading not required.)

Instructions regarding War Diaries and Intelligence Summaries are contained in F. S. Regs., Part II. and the Staff Manual respectively. Title pages will be prepared in manuscript.

Place	Date	Hour	Summary of Events and Information	Remarks and references to Appendices
LA MOTTE AU BOIS	24/9/18		Inspected 2 cases evacuated by 51 M.V.S.	
"	25/9/18		Inspected 7 cases evacuated by 51 M.V.S.	
"	26/9/18		V.O's at Office with returns Inspected 4 cases evacuated by 51 M.V.S.	
"	27/9/18		Sent returns away.	
"	28/9/18		Inspected 5 cases evacuated by 51 M.V.S. Attended G.O.C's conference.	
"	29/9/18		Inspected 6 cases evacuated by 51 M.V.S.	
"	30/9/18		Inspected 10 cases evacuated by 51 M.V.S.	

E Hunt
Capt A.V.C.
a/ADVS, 40th Divn

Army Form C. 2118.

WAR DIARY
or
INTELLIGENCE SUMMARY

(Erase heading not required.) Major W N Proctor D.A.D.V.S. 40th Divn. Oct 1915

Place	Date	Hour	Summary of Events and Information	Remarks and references to Appendices
LE VERRIER	Oct 1		D.H.Q. move to LE VERRIER 36/A20.b.3.4	
"	Oct 2		Returned work from leave	
"	3		All V.O.s & officers until return or inspected clothing estables & 1st Bde & to & plan to inoculations	
"	4		Office work Inspected around 1 S.A.H. section N° V D.A.C submitted report	
"	5		Office work	
"	6		Inoculation 51 MV/S inspected billets, inspection &	
"	7		Inspected around 1/120 Inf Bde submitted report	
"	8		Inspected around of 119 Inf Bde submitted report	
"	9		All V.O.s & officers until return or	
"	10		Inspected around 1 N° V Brigade Co R.E submitted report	

Army Form C. 2118.

WAR DIARY
or
INTELLIGENCE SUMMARY.
(Erase heading not required.)

MARCH
40 Div

Place	Date	Hour	Summary of Events and Information	Remarks and references to Appendices
LEVERRIGNY	11		Wrote ADMS re Corps inspection	
"	12		Inspection interrupted arrival of 330 Bde RFA. Arranged annual of 114 & 4 mnts (Pioneers) & ambulances report. Office routine	
"	13		Went to WALLON CAPPEL & inspected and arranged ambulances arrivals for 40th Div. Undus 51 MVS	
"	14		Undus transport line of 119 M Bde & inspected commat	
"	15		Inspected transport arrangement of 121 M Bde & ambulances report. asst V.O. at Office with return	
"	16		DHQ g move to Avon Ammunition. 51 MVS to 36/H 12 contrd	
ARMENTIERES	17		H.Q. Div Artillery inspection the division	

WAR DIARY
or
INTELLIGENCE SUMMARY.
(Erase heading not required.)

Army Form C. 2118.

Place	Date	Hour	Summary of Events and Information	Remarks and references to Appendices
ARMENTIERES	19		Under 51 M.U.S. Inspected amount of 17th Bn R.F.A.	
	20		51 M.U.S. moves to WAMBRECHIES 36/K.2 cents	
MOUVAUX 31/Friday	21		D.H.Q. move to MOUVAUX (Roubaix)	
"	22		Officers conference. Inspected transp. left behind by the Brode of Arras.	
"	23		Under 51 M.U.S. Inspected billets &c.	
"	24		all O.C.s at H'qrs, rest returns. Officers conference.	
"	25		Under 41 M.U.S.	
	26		Under 41 M.U.S. at Roubaix. Arranged to take over garrison as also by 51 M.U.S. D.H.Q. move to LANNOY (inhab. Roubaix)	
LANNOY	27			

WAR DIARY
or
INTELLIGENCE SUMMARY.

(Erase heading not required.)

Army Form C. 2118.

Place	Date	Hour	Summary of Events and Information	Remarks and references to Appendices
LANNOY	28/10/15		Visited 181 Bde. R.F.A.	
	29/10/15		Inspected I.I.F. arrangements for Div. Artillery & Wednesday. Attended D.D.V.S.'s lecture on the inspection of 149 Bde. R.F.A.	
"	30/10/15		Visited 51 M.V.S. and inspected billets &c.	
	31/10/15		Inspected arrivals of No 6 Div. Train A.S.C. submitted report.	

W.W. Rankin
Major R.A.V.C.

Army Form C. 2118.

WAR DIARY
or
INTELLIGENCE SUMMARY

Major W.N. ROWSTON D.A.D.V.S. 40 Div

November 1918

(Erase heading not required.)

Place	Date	Hour	Summary of Events and Information	Remarks and references to Appendices
LANNOY (M ROUBAIX)	1/11/18		Visited 19 Mob Vet Sec (Rouen) Re input class of mange.	
"	2/11/18		Attended conference at office of A.D.V.S. XV Corps	
			Visited 51 M.V.S. & inspected cases for examination	
"	3/11/18		Inspected animals of 229, 229, 231 Field Coy R.E. submitted report to D.H.Q. (Sub) & A.D.V.S. XV Corps	
"	4/11/18		Inspected animals of Div 102 Section 60 D.A.C. submitted report to D.H.Q. (Sub) & A.D.V.S. XV Corps	
"	5/11/18		Inspected animals of 151 Bde R.F.A. submitted road report	
"	6/11/18		Visited 51 M.V.S. & inspected animals for evacuation	
"	7/11/18		Office routine	
"	8/11/18		Office routine	

WAR DIARY
INTELLIGENCE SUMMARY.
(Erase heading not required.)

Army Form C. 2118.

Place	Date	Hour	Summary of Events and Information	Remarks and references to Appendices
LANNOY	19/11/18		Complete	
"	20/11/18		Respectable description of German attack which has been used by German have suffered from enemy in BEERS	
"	21/11/18		Do Do	
"	22/11/18		No action	
"	23/11/18		Under 51 M.U.S. completed annual auditing inoculation	
"	24/11/18		Routine work	
"	25/11/18		Routine work	
"	26/11/18			

WAR DIARY
or
INTELLIGENCE SUMMARY.
(Erase heading not required.)

Army Form C. 2118.

Place	Date	Hour	Summary of Events and Information	Remarks and references to Appendices
LAVENTIE	18/11/15		WAS went round trench lines of work of 119 Inf Bde	
"	19/11/15		Officers visited	
"	20/11/15		Inspectors arrived of 39th (Amn) M.G. Brigade. Submitted usual report	
"	21/11/15		Inspectors arrived of No 1 Inf Bde & No Wineries (Amn). Submitted usual report. 51 MVS moved to new centres further at CROIX (36/N4d4.7)	
"	22/11/15		Inspectors arrived of No 170 Inf Bde. Submitted usual reports	
"	23/11/15		Inspectors arrived of 119 Inf Bde. Submitted usual reports	
"	24/11/15		Routine work in Office	

WAR DIARY
INTELLIGENCE SUMMARY.

Place	Date	Hour	Summary of Events and Information	Remarks and references to Appendices
ROUBAIX	25/11/18		DHQ move to ROUBAIX (Rue de Lille)	
"	26/11/18		Made a preliminary examination of all men in pelham huts until to return to civilian life upon application for hardin purposes. 2/1/9 Inf Bde 771, 2nd Bn j 14 Warate (Prisoners), S.A.A arrived No 6 D.A.C	
"	27/11/18		Ampules move of D.R.A H.Q. + 1/8 + 1/9 + 1/6/2 Bde R.F.A	
"	28/11/18		Ampules move of No 122 Stalion No D.A.C	
"	29/11/18		Ampules by arrival of 113 Am Pus attch. Bn which arrive here between 1 + 2 p.m. Arrived inspection of 46" Div Art. & Gen. Vaughan. (Ampules of 9 M.G. Branca.)	
"	30/11/18		Ampules move of 120 Inf Bde + 39" M.G. Batt.	

W.W. Rowler
Major Gen

Army Form C. 2118

WAR DIARY or INTELLIGENCE SUMMARY.

MAJOR W.N. ROWSTON DADVS. 40 Div.

(Erase heading not required.)

Place	Date	Hour	Summary of Events and Information	Remarks and references to Appendices
ROUBAIX	1/12/18		Inspected all wagons of 224, 229, 231 Field Coys R.E. and a number of animals of army units for hard work.	
"	2/12/18		Inspected mann of 40 Div Train R.A.S.C. and H.Q. 40 Div.	
"	3/12/18		Inspected mann of 135 & 136 Field Ambulance & 40th Sqdn Cy R.E.	
"	4/12/18		Visited 51 M.V.S. and inspected animals for evacuation. Office routine to A.D.V.O. at Offrin with return.	
"	5/12/18		Visited S.A.A. column 40th D.A.C. & inspected an animal.	
"	6/12/18		Visited 51 M.V.S. and inspected animals for evacuation.	
"	8/12/18		Inspected animals attached to 121 Bde Equivalent Coy at LANNOY.	
"	9/12/18		Inspected all animals 1 A/181 Bde for evidence of mange.	

Army Form C. 2118

WAR DIARY
or
INTELLIGENCE SUMMARY.
(Erase heading not required.)

Instructions regarding War Diaries and Intelligence Summaries are contained in F.S. Regs., Part II. and the Staff Manual respectively. Title pages will be prepared in manuscript.

Place	Date	Hour	Summary of Events and Information	Remarks and references to Appendices
ROUBAIX	10/2/18		Visited 51 M.V.S. and inspected animals for evacuation	
"	11/2/18		Office routine	
	12/2/18		All V.O.'s at Office with return of sick	
"	13/2/18		Attended committee for XV Corps H.Q. at WAMBRECHIES to examine hunt mare, unsound selected	
"	14/2/18		Office routine	
"	15/2/18		Visited 51 M.V.S. and inspected animals for evacuation	
"	16/2/18		Routine work	
"	17/2/18		Routine work	
"	18/2/18		Routine work	

WAR DIARY
or
INTELLIGENCE SUMMARY.

Place	Date	Hour	Summary of Events and Information	Remarks and references to Appendices
ROUBAIX	19/12/18		Attended committee for I.A.H.G. which met first Meeting of hour men	
"	20/12/18		Inspected to arrival of 198 Bde RFA & intensible road report	
"	21/12/18		Inspected RFA horses attached to 40th Div Train	
"	22/12/18		Inspected animals attached to Div Supply Co at MARCQ	
"	23/12/18		Routine work	
"	24/12/18		Visited 51 MVS & inspected animals for evacuation	
"	25/12/18		No duties performed	
"	26/12/18		All V.O.s at office not return &c	

Army Form C. 2118.

WAR DIARY
or
INTELLIGENCE SUMMARY.
(Erase heading not required.)

Place	Date	Hour	Summary of Events and Information	Remarks and references to Appendices
ROUBAIX	29/12/18		Routine work	
"	28/12/18		Attended ADVS conference at IV Corps HQ	
"	29/12/18		Visited 51 MVS and inspected animals for evacuation	
"	30/12/18		Office routine	
"	31/12/18		Inspected & classified & marked all animals 1 A & B Inf Bde. RFA as preliminary to demobilisation	

W W Rankin
Major AVC
DADVS 40 Dn

Army Form C. 2118.

WAR DIARY or INTELLIGENCE SUMMARY

16

D.A.D.V.S. 40 Dn
Major W.W. ROWSTON

No 8 3 3

Place	Date	Hour	Summary of Events and Information	Remarks and references to Appendices
ROUBAIX	1/1/19		Checkfield & amount of R.A. work continued	
"	2/1/19		Ct V.O. at office with returns	
"	3/1/19		Checkfield & amount of R.A. work continued	
"	4/1/19		Checkfield & amount of R.A. work continued	
"	5/1/19		Office routine	
"	6/1/19		Checkfield amount of 40 DAC	
"	7/1/19		Continues checkfields & amount of 40 DAC	
"	8/1/19		Checkfield amount of 22h, 27, 251 Field Coy RE	

WAR DIARY
or
INTELLIGENCE SUMMARY.
(Erase heading not required.)

Army Form C. 2118.

Instructions regarding War Diaries and Intelligence Summaries are contained in F. S. Regs., Part II. and the Staff Manual respectively. Title pages will be prepared in manuscript.

Place	Date	Hour	Summary of Events and Information	Remarks and references to Appendices
ROUBAIX	9/11/19		Routine work	
"	10/11/19		Cleanfeed arrival of No 4 Co Div Train	
"	11/11/19		Cleanfeed arrival with R.A. Agricultural Coy	
"	12/11/19		Cleanfeed arrival with HQrs Agricultural Coy	
"	13/11/19		Cleanfeed arrival with No 1 Co No Div Train	
"	14/11/19		Commence cleanfeed of arrival det 64 AFA Bde	
"	15/11/19		Continue " " "	
"	16/11/19		Routine work & return	
"	17/11/19		Cleanfeed arrival of 119 Inf Bde	

WAR DIARY
or
INTELLIGENCE SUMMARY.

Army Form C. 2118.

Place	Date	Hour	Summary of Events and Information	Remarks and references to Appendices
ROUBAIX	18/11/19			
	19/11/19		Classified annual of 120 Inf Bde	
	20/11/19		Classified annual of 203 Coy MC Dn Train	
	21/11/19		Classified annual of 121 Inf Bde & 19" Ward (Prumi)	
	22/11/19		Classified annual of 59 Army M. Gun Batt.	
	23/11/19		Classified annual of 40" Sigul Cy RE	
			Officer routine & returns	
	24/11/19		Classified annual of 135, 136, 139 Field Ambulances	
	25/11/19		Classified annual of CRE. H.Q. & 51 MUS	
	26/11/19		Routine and	
	27/11/19		Routine work & inspection of welfare testing	

Army Form C. 2118.

WAR DIARY
or
INTELLIGENCE SUMMARY.
(Erase heading not required.)

Instructions regarding War Diaries and Intelligence Summaries are contained in F. S. Regs., Part II. and the Staff Manual respectively. Title pages will be prepared in manuscript.

Place	Date	Hour	Summary of Events and Information	Remarks and references to Appendices
ROUBAIX	28/1/19		Visited 64 AFA Bde to inspect mobilised animals	
"	29/1/19		Accompanied DD Vet A.S. Remount Board	
"	30/1/19		Attended conference at A.D.V.S. DD Vet A.S.	
"	30/1/19		Accompanied DD Vet A.S. Remount Board	

W.W. Rumbu
Major RAVC
D.A.D.V.S. 40 Div

Army Form C. 2118.

WAR DIARY
of MAJOR W.N. ROWSTON or PADMS 40 Dn
INTELLIGENCE SUMMARY.
(Erase heading not required.) Feb. 1919

Place	Date	Hour	Summary of Events and Information	Remarks and references to Appendices
ROUBAIX	1/2/19		Medical cases of D.H.Q. & 40" Signal Co selected for early repatriation to England	
"	2/2/19		Routine work, visited 51 MVS	
"	3/2/19		Routine work	
"	4/2/19		Routine work	
"	5/2/19		Inspected 40 Div horse mule and &c & found additions to 51 MVS evacuation & forwarded report on same to ADVS XI Corps as few of the animals collected on arrival of the remounts which are now on pet to change to fresh unit to be evacuated to hosp.	
"	6/2/19		Issued order to 51 MVS that Divnl horses now not to be accepted unless in a fit state to be evacuated. Div Divnl horses evacuated to 51 MVS	

Army Form C. 2118.

WAR DIARY
or
INTELLIGENCE SUMMARY.
(Erase heading not required.)

Instructions regarding War Diaries and Intelligence Summaries are contained in F. S. Regs., Part II. and the Staff Manual respectively. Title pages will be prepared in manuscript.

Place	Date	Hour	Summary of Events and Information	Remarks and references to Appendices
ROUBAIX	7/2/19		Routine work	
"	8/2/19		2 Trucks from recruits to 51 MVS	
			Routine work	
			2 Trucks horses removed to 51 MVS	
"	9/2/19		Routine work	
"	10/2/19		Under H.Q. VII Corps to arrange mulemen & animals for cadre	
"	11/2/19		Mulemen animals & mules of VII Corps for cadre in repatriation to England	
"	12/2/19		Inspector animals mulemen	
			Routine work.	
"	13/2/19		Inspector animals made mulemen tests	
			All V.O.'s at Mons went advance	
"	14/2/19		Capt H. made O.C. 51 MVS went to A. Gardeluu mulemen from influenza half were in MVS all down with influenza 1 or 2 life & serv in camp in	

WAR DIARY
or
INTELLIGENCE SUMMARY.

Army Form C. 2118.

Place	Date	Hour	Summary of Events and Information	Remarks and references to Appendices
ROUBAIX	15/2/19		Capt Hanel RAMC took over S: MVS as a temporary measure thanks an arrival of report arrival to him	
"	18/2/19		Visited 39 Machine Gun Bn	
"	19/2/19		Visited 51 MVS	
"	18/2/19		Office routine	
"	19/2/19		Visited 51 MVS	
"			of J.O. at office usual return	
"	20/2/19		Routine work	
"	21/2/19		Routine work	
"	22/2/19		Visited 51 MVS	
"	23/2/19		Capt Huntley O.C. Signals remained to form school M strength	
"			Refer instr. number 231 Field A RE	
"	25/2/19		Routine work	
"	26/2/19		"	
"	27/2/19		Visited Hospitals, Annual of work of 147 Fd Bt, 224 Fd A RE, 775 Fd A RE	
"	28/2/19			
			WN Rowlin Major RAMC DADVS 74 Dn	

Army Form C. 2118.

WAR DIARY or INTELLIGENCE SUMMARY.

Major ROWSTON DADVS 40 Dⁿ

March 1919

(Erase heading not required.)

Place	Date	Hour	Summary of Events and Information	Remarks and references to Appendices
ROUBAIX	1/3/19		Proceeded to H.Q. XII Corps to act Temporarily as ADVS pending arrival of the new ADVS	
"	2/3/19		Routine duties at Corps DnHQ	
"	3/3/19		" "	
"	4/3/19		Lt Col Verny Coxd arrived & took over duties of ADVS Corps. Returned to Dn. HQ	
"	5/3/19		Routine work	
"	6/3/19		All VO's at office with return etc	
"	7/3/19		Routine work	
"	8/3/19		The strength of animals in 40ᵗʰ Dn is now a little over 6 thousand and consequently there is little to be done. The strength of the 51 AVS is now reduced to 4 O.R.	

Army Form C. 2118.

WAR DIARY
or
INTELLIGENCE SUMMARY.
(Erase heading not required.)

Place	Date	Hour	Summary of Events and Information	Remarks and references to Appendices
Rendcomb	8/3/19		The equipment of 51 MUS has been checked & made up to mobilization store table & the unit is ready to become a cadre unit.	
	9/3/19		Routine work, orders have been issued for and surplus m/t equipment and stores to be handed in to 51 MUS for return to the base. Routine work	
	10/3/19			
	11			
	12			
	13			
	14			
	15			
	16		Self to go on leave.	

WN Rendin
Major OC

www.ingramcontent.com/pod-product-compliance
Lightning Source LLC
Chambersburg PA
CBHW081533160426
43191CB00011B/1747